HANDBOOK AND GUIDE FOR COMPARING and SELECTING COMPUTER LANGUAGES

BASIC	PL/1
FORTRAN	APL
PASCAL	ALGOL-60
COBOL	C

**Staff of Research and Education Association,
Dr. M. Fogiel, Director**

Research and Education Association
505 Eighth Avenue
New York, N. Y. 10018

HANDBOOK AND GUIDE FOR COMPARING AND
SELECTING COMPUTER LANGUAGES

Printed in the United States of America

Library of Congress Catalog Card Number 84-61817

International Standard Book Number 0-87891-561-3

Revised Printing, 1987

PREFACE

In recent years large numbers of programming languages have been made available through the efforts of persons in computer science. Although most of these languages can be used for one application or another, a great deal of confusion exists as to which language is most appropriate for a given application. From among the various languages that have been developed, eight languages remain as the most practical and advantageous to use. These are BASIC, FORTRAN, PASCAL, COBOL, PL/1, APL, ALGOL-60, and C.

Although the vast number of available programming languages can be largely narrowed down to these eight languages, the programmer is left, nonetheless, with the difficult task of choosing the language that is most suitable for the given purpose.

This book is intended to help the programmer in making the correct choice by showing the similarities and differences that exist among these eight most important languages. The book is arranged to enable the programmer to compare all eight languages at a glance, for any given aspect or feature. This makes it possible for the programmer to weigh the pro's and con's rapidly and from that select the most appropriate language.

This book also enables the reader who has a fundamental background in programming to (1) learn new languages, and to (2) design a new language. Transition from one language to another is readily achieved with the use of this book.

CONTENTS

FACTORS IN THE CHOICE OF A LANGUAGE

Factors that should be taken into account when selecting an appropriate language for problem solving are:

1. Clarity, simplicity and unity of language.

A programming language provides both a conceptual framework for thinking about algorithms and a means of expressing these algorithms for machine execution. The language should be an aid to the programmer long before he reaches the actual coding stage in programming. It should also provide him with a clear, simple and unified set of concepts so that it can be used initially in developing algorithms. The language must be unambiguous. It is this semantic clarity, i.e., clarity of concept, which is the most significant factor in selecting a language.

2. Clarity of program structure. Closely related to but quite different from the idea of semantic clarity of a language is the concept of syntactic clarity of programs written in the language. The syntax of a language greatly affects the ease with which a program may be written, tested, and later understood and modified. Many languages contain syntactic constructions which are likely to lead to programming errors. At best such constructions lead to trivial syntax errors caught during translation. A language should have the property that constructs, which means different things look different; i.e., semantic differences should be mirrored syntactically. Additionally, it is extremely useful to allow minor but obvious variations in the way a statement is written.

3. Naturalness of the application. The language should provide appropriate data structures, operations, control structures and a natural syntax for the problem to be solved. One of the major reasons for the proliferation of languages is just this need for naturalness. A language particularly suited (in both syntax and semantics) to a certain class of applications may greatly simplify the creation of individual programs in that area.

4. Ease of extension. A substantial part of the programmer's task in constructing any large set of programs may be viewed as language extension. The language should allow extension through simple, natural and elegant mechanisms.

5. External support. The technical structure of a programming language and its implementation is only one aspect affecting its utility. The presence of complete and usable documentation and a tested and error-free implementation are also strong determinants of the utility of a language.

An important question in many large programming tasks is that of the transportability of the resultant set of programs. A language which is widely available and whose definition is independent of the features of a particular machine forms a useful base for the production of transportable programs.

6. Efficiency. Efficiency is certainly a major element in the evaluation of any programming language. There is a variety of different measures of efficiency.

a. Efficiency of program execution. Efficiency of program execution, although always of some importance in language design, is of primary importance for large production programs which will be executed many times.

b. Efficiency of program translation. In certain languages, the question of efficient translation (compilation) rather than efficient execution may be paramount. In such a case it is important to have a fast and efficient compiler rather than a compiler which produces optimized executable code.

c. Efficiency of program creation, testing and use. This is a third aspect of efficiency in a programming language. For a certain class of problems, a solution may be designed, coded, tested, and modified with a minimum waste of the programmer's time and energy.

Choosing the best language for a problem solving task can be a difficult assignment. This book, we feel, should aid in the difficult task of language selection.

OVERVIEW OF THE LANGUAGES

BASIC

INTRODUCTION

BASIC (Beginner's All-purpose Symbolic Instruction Code) was developed in the early 1960's at Dartmouth College to make the computer more accessible and easy to use both by students and faculty. One of the objectives was to develop a language that could be learned quickly, and was powerful enough to be used in solving problems from small scale to medium scale in any discipline.

BASIC statements and operands are very close to both actual English language and algebra, and is also very easy to comprehend. This has ensured its popularity in almost all fields of science, business and engineering.

A lot of improved versions of BASIC have been developed like BASICA Applesoft BASIC, C BASIC, Microsoft BASIC, etc. Microsoft BASIC (developed for CP/M-based systems) is probably the most powerful BASIC language available at this time.

BRIEF OVERVIEW OF THE LANGUAGE

The language was designed to be very simple to learn and easy to translate. BASIC is commonly available on time sharing systems, and is widely implemented on mini- and micro-computer systems.

A BASIC program consists of a single block of numbered statements. Functions and subroutines are within this main block. No independent sub-programs are allowed.

The standard data types are numeric and string. The standard structured data types are the array, the record and the sequential file.

In BASIC, statement sequence control is achieved through GOTO, ON-GOTO, FOR-NEXT, and IF-THEN statements. The READ statement is used to read data from the corresponding DATA statement. The most commonly used output statement is the PRINT statement. The GOSUB is the subroutine call. Functions are invoked by writing the function name, followed by the parameters enclosed in parentheses.

BASIC also contains matrix manipulation and file handling statements, with a self contained set of system commands.

FORTRAN

INTRODUCTION

FORTRAN (FORmula TRANslation) was the first widely used high level programming language. The earliest versions were designed and implemented in the mid 1950's.

Since its introduction, features have been steadily added to the language. The latest version is FORTRAN-77. FORTRAN is a computer programming language which resembles elementary algebra, augmented by certain English words such as DO, GO TO, READ, WRITE, IF, etc. Because of its similarity to ordinary algebra, the FORTRAN language is well suited for solving problems in science, mathematics, and engineering. However, use of the language is by no means restricted to these areas. FORTRAN is also applied to a wide variety of problems in business, economics, psychology, medicine, library science-- virtually any area requiring extensive manipulation of numerical data or character information. Such a large number of areas of application together with simplicity of learning and usage, makes FORTRAN the most popular computer language.

The standard data types are those of integer, real, double precision and complex numbers, and logical and literal values. In FORTRAN, the input and output data has to be formatted, always. The input format statements specify the form in which data has to be stored in the memory. The output format statement specifies the form in which data has to be written onto an output device. The only structured data type is the multi-dimensional array. Fortran statement sequence control depends heavily on GO TO statement label structures. Subprogram sequence control is the basic CALL and RETURN structure without recursion.

BRIEF OVERVIEW OF THE LANGUAGE

The language was designed with the primary goal of execution efficiency. The language structures are simple, and much of the design is rather inelegant, but the goal of execution efficiency is achieved. FORTRAN can be implemented on most computers so that execution is extremely efficient, using hardware structures directly for almost everything except input-output. The simplicity of structures and execution efficiency make it ideal for scientific computing.

A FORTRAN program consists of a main program and a set of separately compiled subprograms, with translated subprograms linked together during loading. No run time storage management is provided. Subprograms can only communicate by accessing COMMON storage, passing parameters and passing control through non-recursive subprogram calls. Thus the run time structure of a FORTRAN program is static.

PASCAL

INTRODUCTION

Pascal is the most important contribution to programming in the recent past. Pascal was invented by Prof. Niklaus Wirth of Zurich in 1970 for two reasons. Firstly, "...to make available a language suitable to teach programming as a systematic discipline based on certain fundamental concepts, clearly and naturally reflected by the language.", and secondly, "...to develop implementations of this language, which are both reliable and efficient on presently available computers.".

In American and European institutions of higher learning, Pascal is fast becoming a major computer teaching language due to the desirable features of the language and the ease of producing an efficient compiler. The use of Pascal is growing rapidly in a wide field of applications--from first course teaching to microprocessor and system programming.

All objects such as constants, variables, procedures etc must be declared before they are referenced. There are only two exceptions:

1) the type identifier in a pointer type definition.
2) procedure and function calls when there is a forward reference.

Statement sequence control in Pascal includes statement label-GO TO structure, If-THEN-ELSE, REPEAT-UNTIL, WHILE-DO, FOR-DOWN TO, FOR-TO, and CASE constructs. Pascal allows procedures and functions to be called with recursion.

BRIEF OVERVIEW OF THE LANGUAGE

A Pascal program is composed of a data definition section (for constants, labels, types and variables), executable block definitions (procedures and functions), and an executable 'main' program block. All Pascal programs begin with the 'reserved' word PROGRAM. This is then followed by a program name and an input/output specification. The 'main' block is the outermost program-defined block which is the first block executed when the program is run.

The standard data types are those of integer and real numbers, logical values, and the printable characters. The basic data structuring facilities include the ARRAY, the RECORD, the SET and the sequential FILE. These structures can be combined and nested to form arrays of sets, files of records, etc. Data may be allocated dynamically and accessed via pointers. There is also a facility to declare new, basic data types with symbolic constants. The above described feature of powerful type extensionability is Pascal's most significant feature.

COBOL

INTRODUCTION

COBOL (COmmon Business-Oriented Language) was developed in the late 1950's to provide a relatively machine-independent language for solving business data processing problems. An early version of the COBOL language appeared in December, 1959. It was then followed by COBOL-61, which has provided the basis for the development of later versions. The next version was developed in 1965. However, it was not until August, 1968 that a standard version was approved by the American National Standards Institute (ANSI). This standard version ANSI COBOL was again revised in 1974, and has now been implemented by all major manufacturers and most well-managed installations.

Business data processing has a somewhat unique character--relatively simple algorithms coupled with high volume input-output (e.g, computing the payroll for a large organization). Because input-output is a prime concern for business data processing, COBOL is designed with emphasis on features for specification of the properties and structure of input-output files.

BRIEF OVERVIEW OF THE LANGUAGE

Every COBOL program is organized into four divisions, with the primary goals of separating machine-dependent from machine-independent program elements, and that of separating data descriptions from algorithm descriptions, so that each may be modified without affecting the other. The result is the following program organization: the PROCEDURE DIVISION which includes the algorithms, the DATA DIVISION which contains the data descriptions, the ENVIRONMENT DIVISION which specifies the machine-dependent input-output devices to be used, and the IDENTIFICATION DIVISION which begins the program and serves to identify it and its author. This also helps in providing program documentation.

The basic elementary data types are numbers and character strings, with the basic data structure being the record. Records are also the basis of external data file structures, which are very important in COBOL. The structures of array and record can be combined and nested to form arrays of records and records of arrays. All structures must be fully declared along with type declarations of all data elements in the DATA DIVISION.

Built-in operations include simple arithmetic, logical and relational operations, and simple character scanning and substitution. Other features include automatic type conversion, and a powerful set of input-output verbs for accessing and manipulating external files. These include input-output for sequential, indexed sequential, and random access files; a SORT feature, a report writer feature, a segmentation feature, and a source program library feature.

COBOL statement sequence control includes a statement label GO TO structure, IF-THEN-ELSE construct and a PERFORM statement.

The language has an English-like syntax which provides good self-documentation. However, the syntax makes writing even the simplest program a fairly lengthy process.

PL/1

INTRODUCTION

PL/1 (Programming Language 1) is a multi-purpose programming language. It was designed to be used by both scientific and commercial programmers. PL/1 is a product of a team set up by the Share organization of FORTRAN users. The initial goal was to design a successor to FORTRAN which would include more extensive data structuring facilities.

PL/1 is constructed so that the individual programmer can program at his own level of experience, whether high or low. The language has many automatic and default conditions to assist the beginner, while the experienced programmer may detail each and every step of his complicated program. Unfortunately the default condition concept, in practice, sometimes is more confusing than helpful to the programmer, as the condition may not be that which is expected.

BRIEF OVERVIEW OF THE LANGUAGE

A PL/1 program consists of one or more separately compiled external procedures. Each external procedure is constructed from units which are one of the following:

1) simple statements
2) compound statements
3) DO groups
4) BEGIN blocks
5) internal procedures

Internal and external procedures are identical syntactically but differ in that any variable in the external procedure is accessible to the internal procedure. The converse is not true.

PL/1 contains a wide variety of elementary data types, including an extensive set of possible type specifications for numeric data. Character strings, bit strings, labels, and pointers can also be used. However, there is no Boolean/logical data type. Instead, a bit string of length 1 is used. The basic structuring facilities are the homogeneous and hetrogeneous arrays. These may be combined and

nested as in COBOL. Full declarations are necessary. Built-in operations include simple arithmetic, relational and simple character scanning, retrieval, and concatenation. Other features include automatic type conversion, and a powerful set of input-output verbs for accessing and manipulating external files, which may be of record or stream type. Record files may be structured as sequential, indexed sequential or random access. Stream files are sequential.

PL/1 statement sequence control includes statement label GO TO structure, IF-THEN-ELSE construct, DO construct, etc. Subprogram sequence control includes the basic CALL-RETURN structure, with recursion if the subprogram has been specifically declared recursive in its definition. The language also has novel features for parallel processing and interrupt handling.

The language is complex and is not easy to read or write. Its wide versatility makes it a relatively harder language to learn in its entirety.

APL

INTRODUCTION

APL (A Programming Language) was defined by Kenneth Iverson. Widely recognized as a scientific language, APL is equally useful in business, education, finance and many other fields. A modified version of the original language, termed APL/360, was implemented in the late 1960's. Several enhanced versions of APL, such as IBM APL2, have been introduced in recent years. These implementations of the language incorporate many powerful extensions, such as the support of heterogeneous nested arrays (mixed numeric and character) as well as mixed array rank.

APL is a versatile programming language providing a direct means of problem solving by students, engineers, scientists, educators, and businessmen. It is used interactively on a computer terminal. The power and conciseness of the language make it well suited to the interactive environment, because a line of only a few characters typed on the terminal can do a surprising amount of computation. The language is much less suitable for construction of large programs to be used repeatedly for production computing.

Being a versatile language, it can be used in either execution or definition modes. In execution mode the language enables one to operate the terminal as though it were a desk calculator. In definition mode one is able to enter, store, execute and debug programs. APL is efficient when compared with other languages. It takes the least amount of programming effort to accomplish a given job. When in execution mode, APL has immediate diagnostics. The system reports errors as soon as they are made, and gives their type and location. All of these features make APL a strong tool in solving a wide range of complicated problems.

BRIEF OVERVIEW OF THE LANGUAGE

APL is based on simple homogeneous array data structures of type number or character. Typing is strictly dynamic, and of no direct concern to the programmer (except for the fact that certain operators apply only to arrays of numbers). A large class of primitive operators are built-in, including many which create, destroy, and modify arrays. Every APL primitive is defined as a function which returns a value. APL control structures are quite simple. Within expressions there is no hierarchy of operations, and right-to-left association is used in place of the more usual left-to-right technique. There is no concept of a main program in APL. Subprogram execution is initiated either by a call from another subprogram, or by the programmer at his terminal, through entry and execution of an expression containing a function call. In the latter case, control returns to the programmer at the terminal after subprogram execution is complete. In a sense, the programmer creates and executes the main program line by line during a session at the terminal.

Between statements and subprograms, all that is provided is a simple goto, which allows a computed statement number and recursive subprogram calls. Moreover, various kinds of interruptions may be set to break into program execution and return control to the programmer at his terminal, allowing the programmer to enter new data, modify old data values, or modify the program before restarting the interrupted program at a designated statement.

Subprograms are restricted to no more than two arguments transmitted by value and a single result. However, arguments and result can be scalar, vector, or higher order dimensional arrays of numeric or character data. Therefore, APL is less restrictive than most other languages in this respect. Subprograms have the form of a simple sequence of statements, each of which has a system-generated line number and which may, in addition, have a programmer-supplied label. Goto statements may designate their object either by a line number or a statement label.

APL has perhaps the most extensively specified operating environment of any language. This environment of course includes the programmer at his terminal. For external storage, programs and data are grouped into workspace; these may be saved from session to session by the programmer. Each workspace may contain various programs and data structures, including partially written programs and programs that have been partially executed and then interrupted. System commands are provided to allow workspaces to be brought into central memory from external storage, and stored back again after being updated. In addition, subprogram definitions and data structures may be transferred individually by name between a stored workspace and the currently active one.

(Continued on page 8)

APL

A typical APL implementation is based on purely software interpreted program execution. Two static storage areas are allocated, one for system routines and one for the workspace currently in use by the programmer. The system routines are ordinarily shared between several users, each with his own workspace area. The workspace area contains some static storage for system data and three dynamic storage areas: a stack for subprogram activation records, a heap for array storage and storage of the bodies of defined subprograms, and a table of global identifier associations. Arrays are stored with full run-time descriptors in usual sequential simulation.

ALGOL-60

INTRODUCTION

ALGOL-60 (Algorithmic Language) was designed by an international committee during the late 1950's and early 1960's. The definition of ALGOL-60 was a key event in the history of programming languages. No other single language has had such far-reaching influence on the design and definition of languages. ALGOL has also been the central language on which much research in programming languages has been based.

ALGOL is usually classified as a language for scientific computations because of its emphasis on numeric data and homogeneous array data structures.

Two outstanding characteristics make ALGOL important: first, the general clarity and elegance of its structure, and the manner of its definition. Of particular note are its control structures; both PL/1 and later versions of FORTRAN have been benefited from ALGOL control structure design, as have many other languages, e.g., BLISS and Pascal. A successor to ALGOL, the language ALGOL-88, was designed by another committee. Secondly, that it has served for many years as the primary publication language for algorithms in the communications of the ACM and other journals. A knowledge of ALGOL is now a necessary prerequisite to much advanced work in programming languages and related areas.

BRIEF OVERVIEW OF THE LANGUAGE

ALGOL is a language designed for compilation. In the usual implementation, programs and subprograms are compiled into machine code, with only a minimum of software simulation required for some of the primitive operations. Owing to the dynamic storage allocation and referencing environment, updating is necessary during execution. ALGOL programs in general cannot be executed as efficiently as equivalent FORTRAN programs on conventional hardware. This is one major reason why ALGOL has never supplanted FORTRAN in much of scientific programming.

An ALGOL program is composed of a main program and a set of subprograms constructed of blocks. A block is composed of a set of declarations followed by a sequence of statements, with the whole block enclosed by the delimit begin...end. The main program is simply a single block. Each subprogram definition is composed of a header, which declares the subprogram name, and the names of the formal parameters, and types for each name, and a body, which in general is a block.

The statements within a block center around the usual assignment statement, which may be used to assign new values to simple variables or elements of arrays. The other statement types that are used for sequence control are:

a test-branch-join conditional statement, an iteration statement, a subprogram call statement, an iteration statement, a subprogram (with recursion), and statement labels and a goto statement. In addition, one block may appear as a statement within another block, which allows the definition of new identifier associations and new data structures at any point. Such associations are local to the block, and may not be referenced outside the block in which they occur.

Data is ALGOL is restricted to simple homogeneous arrays of integer, real, or Boolean elements. A fairly extensive set of arithmetic, relational, and logical operations are provided. ALGOL is the original block-structured language, using the static structure to determine referencing environments throughout.

The language provides two options for transmission of actual parameters to subprograms: transmission by value, and transmission by name.

C

INTRODUCTION

C is a general-purpose programming language, originally designed for and implemented on the UNIX operating system on the DEC PDP-11. (UNIX is a trademark for Bell Laboratories). The C language has been closely associated with the UNIX system, since it was developed on that system and since UNIX and its software are written in C. The language, however, is not tied to any one operating system or machine; although it has been called a "system programming language" because it is useful for writing operating systems, it has been used equally well to write major numerical, text processing, and data-base programs. Thus, its absence of restrictions and its generality makes it more convenient and effective for many tasks than supposedly more powerful languages. The operating system, the C compiler, and essentially all UNIX application programs are written in C. Production compilers also exist for several other machines, including the IBM system/370, the Honeywell 6000, and the Interdata 8/32.

BRIEF OVERVIEW OF THE LANGUAGE

C is a relatively "low level" language. This characterization is not perjorative; it simply means that C deals with the same sort of objects that most computers do, namely characters, numbers and addresses. These may be combined and moved about with the usual arithmetic and logical operators implemented by actual machines.

C provides no operations to deal directly with composite objects such as character strings, sets, lists, or arrays considered as a whole. The language does not define any storage allocation facility other than static definition and the stack discipline provided by the local variables of functions. There is no heap or garbage collection like that provided by ALGOL-68. Finally, C itself provides no input-output facilities. There are no READ or WRITE statements and no wired-in file access methods. All of these higher-level mechanisms must be provided by explicitly-called functions. C offers only straightforward single-thread control flow constructions: tests, loops, group-ing and subprograms, but not multi-programming, parallel operations, synchronization or co-routines. Since C is relatively small, it can be described in a small space and learned quickly. A compiler for C can be simple and compact. Compilers are also easily written: using current technology, one can expect to prepare a compiler for a new machine in a couple of months, and to find that 80 percent of the code of a new compiler is common with existing ones. This provides a high degree of language mobility. Because the data types and control structures provided by C are supported directly by most existing computers, the run-time library required to implement self-contained programs is tiny. Again, because the language reflects the capabilities of current computers, C programs tend to be efficient enough that there is no compulsion to write assembly language instead. Although C matches the capabilities of many computers, it is independent of any particular machine architecture. With a little care, it is easy to write "portable" programs, that is, programs which can be run without much change on a variety of hardware.

In C, the fundamental objects are characters, integers of several sizes, and floating point numbers. In addition, there is a hierarchy of derived data types created with pointers, arrays, structures, unions and functions.

C provides the fundamental flow control constructions required for well-structured programs such as statement grouping, decision making (if), looping with the termination test at the top (while, for) or at the bottom (do), and selecting one of the sets of possible cases (switch). C provides pointers, and the ability to do address arithmetic. The arguments to functions are passed by copying the value of the argument, and it is impossible for the called function to change the actual argument in the caller. When it is desired to achieve "call by reference", a pointer may be passed explicitly, and the function may change the object to which the pointer points. Array names are passed as the location of the array origin, so array arguments are effectively called by reference.

Any function may be called recursively and its local variables are typically "automatic", or created with each invocation. Function definition may not be nested, but variables may be declared in a block-structured fashion. The functions of a C program may be compiled separately. Variables may be internal to a function or external, but known only within a single source file, or completely global. Internal variables may be automatic or static. Automatic variables may be placed in registers for increased efficiency, but the register declaration is only a hint to the compiler, and does not refer to specific machine registers.

C is not a strongly-typed language in the sense of Pascal or Algol-68. It is relatively permissive about data conversion, although it will not automatically convert data types with the wild abandon of PL/1. Existing compilers provide no run-time checking of array subscripts, argument types, etc.

Finally, C, like any other language, has its blemishes. Some of the operators have the wrong precedence, some parts of the syntax could be better, and there are several versions of the language, differing in minor ways. Nonetheless, C has proven to be an extremely effective and expressive language for a wide variety of programming applications.

COMPARISON OF THE LANGUAGES

1. PROGRAM STRUCTURE

BASIC

The BASIC program structure is a single block of statements with increasing statement numbers. Functions and subroutines are a part of the program block.

FORTRAN

The FORTRAN program structure consists of a main program and a number of separately compiled functions and/or subroutine subprograms. Each subprogram is an independent FORTRAN program which can transfer data to and from its calling program.

PL/1

A PL/1 program consists of one or more separately compiled external PROCEDURE blocks. Each external PROCEDURE block is constructed from one of the following: DO groups, BEGIN blocks and internal PROCEDURE blocks. Each PROCEDURE block is contained between a PROCEDURE and an END statement. The internal PROCEDURE block is syntactically identical to the external PROCEDURE block. A BEGIN block is a sequence of statements between the words BEGIN and END. Internal PROCEDURE blocks and BEGIN blocks can be nested.

APL

Every APL program has four main parts; the beginning, the header, the body and the ending. In APL, there is no concept of a main program. Subprogram execution is initiated by either calls from other subprograms or by programmer at his terminal through entry and execution of an expression containing a function call. In APL, Del (∇) constitutes the beginning of the program. Its function is to change the mode of operation from execution mode to definition mode. Execution mode is sometimes referred to as desk calculator mode, while definition mode is referred to as programming mode. When the system is in programming mode, each instruction is entered and stored in the workspace. Later, when the program is called to run, each instruction is executed in sequence. The name of the program is the header. The body of the program contains APL instructions that direct the computer to accomplish its various tasks. The ending ∇, returns the system to execution mode.

PASCAL

The first word of all Pascal programs is PROGRAM. This is followed by a program name and an Input/Output specification. Every Pascal program is composed of a data definition section (for constants, labels, types and variables), executable block definitions (procedures and functions) and an executable main program block. The main program block is the first block to be executed when the program is run. The declarations in the block are optional but if both are present then constant declarations must precede the variable declarations. Procedures may be nested and can be called recursively.

COBOL

Every COBOL program is organized into four divisions. (IDENTIFICATION DIVISION, ENVIRONMENT DIVISION, DATA DIVISION and PROCEDURE DIVISION). The last three divisions are further organized into sections which contain sentences and paragraphs. Sections and paragraphs in the PROCEDURE DIVISION that can be used as simple subprograms can be called by a PERFORM statement. ANSI COBOL-74 includes independent subprograms or subroutines.

ALGOL-60

A complete ALGOL program may consist of a main program and a number of self-contained program segments called procedures. Procedures may be written as functions or as subroutines, allowing data to be transferred to and from their invoking or calling program segment. Each independent program segment will be comprised of one or more blocks of statements. A block is a sequence of statements contained between the words BEGIN and END. Declarations must be included within each block. Blocks can be nested.

C

A C program generally consists of numerous small "functions" (rather than a few big ones) which specify the actual computing operations that are to be done. A program may reside on one or more source files in any convenient way; the source files may be compiled separately and loaded together along with previously compiled functions from libraries. C functions are similar to the functions and subroutines of a Fortran program or the procedures of PL/1, Pascal, etc. Normally you are at liberty to give functions whatever names you like, but main is a special name -- your program begins executing at the beginning of main. This means that every program must have a main somewhere. Main will usually invoke other functions to perform its job, some coming from the same program, and others from libraries of previously written functions. The braces { } enclose the statements that make up the function; they are analogous to the DO-END of PL/1 or the begin-end of Algol and Pascal.

2. STATEMENT LAYOUT

BASIC

Only one line per statement is allowed but multiple statements can appear in a single line. Statements are executed in ascending order of their line numbers, with the exception of GO TO and GO SUB statements.

Examples

```
10   INPUT  F
20   LET C=(F-32)/1.8
30   PRINT "TEMPERATURE IS"; C
```

FORTRAN

Only columns 7-72 can be used, with continuation from one card (line) to another by having a character other than a blank or zero in column 6. Columns 1-5 are reserved for statement numbers. All Fortran statements need not be numbered. Statements which will be referred to within the program have to be numbered.

Examples

```
     DC=(DF-32.)/1.8
30   WRITE (6,3)  DC
 3   FORMAT ('TEMPERATURE IS' ,F6.2)
```

PL/1

Statements are written in free form with any number of spaces and/or new lines used to separate words and symbols. Labels are optional and must end with a colon. Each statement is terminated with a semicolon. A BEGIN block starts with the word BEGIN and ends with the word END.

Example

```
Statement:
DC=(DF-32.0)/1.8;

Begin Block:
SOLN:  BEGIN;
C=SQRT(A**2+B**2-2*A*B*COS(ALPHA));
S=1/2*(A+B+C);
AREA=SQRT(S*(S-A)*(S-B)*(S-C));
END;
```

APL

Each subprogram statement has a system generated line number and may have programmer defined label. Each statement must be seperated from the next by a semicolon or the diamond symbol ◇. These seperators are only needed when there are two or more statements on one line.

Example

```
     ∇I SUM
[1]  'SUM of 1ST 100 INTEGERS:';+/100∇
```

Thus in APL there is no compound statement (as in ALGOL-60, Pascal) which starts with the word BEGIN and ends with the word END.

14

PASCAL

Each statement must be specifically separated from the next by a semicolon, except the statement just before the END statement. Compound statements start with the reserved word BEGIN and end with the reserved word END.

Examples

Simple Statement:
```
DC:=(DF-32.0)/1.8;
WRITELN('TEMPERATURE IS',DC);
```

Compound Statement:
```
BEGIN
C:=SQRT(SQR(A)+SQR(B)-2*A*B*COS(ALPHA));
S:=1/2*(A+B+C);
AREA:=SQRT(S*(S-A)*(S-B)*(S-C))
END;
```

COBOL

Only columns 8-72 can be used, with continuation from one card (line) to another by placing a hyphen in column 7. A statement consists of identifiers, keywords and clauses that are used to form sentences. Each sentence is terminated with a period followed by a blank space.

Example

Statement:
```
ADD SALARY-IN TO MEN-TOTAL-SALARY
```

ALGOL-60

There are two types of statements. One is a simple statement written in free form but must end with a semicolon. Labels are optional and must end with a colon. The other is a compound statement which starts with the word BEGIN and ends with the word END.

Examples

Simple statement:
```
CALC:DC:=(F-32)/1.8
```

Compound statement:
```
BEGIN
C:=SQRT(A↑2+B↑2-2*A*B*COS(ALPHA));
S:=1/2*(A+B+C);
AREA:=SQRT(S*(S-A)*(S-B)*(S-C))
END;
```

C

Written in free form with any number of spaces and/or new lines used to separate the words and symbols. Each statement must be specifically separated from the next by a semicolon. A C program always starts with a left-brace { and ends with a right brace } . Braces can be used within these braces, just like BEGIN and END in ALGOL, Pascal and so on. Thus C statements are compound rather than simple.

Example

```
{
celsius=(5.0/9.0)*(fahr-32.0);
print f ("%4.0f%6.1f\n";fahr,celsius);
fahr=fahr + step;
}
```

3. ELEMENTARY DATA TYPES

BASIC

Type	Examples
Numeric:	124, 10001, -1.276E-5
String:	"JACK", "$125.60"

It is important to mention here that numeric and string are the data types of standard BASIC. Some powerful versions of BASIC such as the Microsoft BASIC 5.0 have single precision and double precision data types also.

FORTRAN

Type	Examples
INTEGER:	124, 10001, -102, +576
REAL:	1.276, -1027., 1.276E-14
DOUBLE PRECISION:	1.276D-14
COMPLEX:	(5.21, -3.1)
LOGICAL:	.TRUE., .FALSE.
LITERAL:	'JACK', 4HJACK
CHARACTER: (FORTRAN 77)	'A', '9'

PL/1

Type	Examples
ARITHMETIC: (Binary/Decimal fixed or floating point)	1011011, .001, 89 101101E5, -1.44E-5
Character-String:	'JACK' 'DISCOUNT'
Bit-String:	'101101'
Statement-Label:	STEP1:
Entry:	ARITH6
File:	FILE3

APL

APL is quite restricted in its data-structuring facilities. Numbers and single characters are elementary data types. APL handles numeric data (fixed and floating), integer, logical (boolean) or character data with equal ease and facility. APL2 (and similar variants) handle complex numbers intrinsically.

Type	Examples
Numeric:	8, 3623, -45, 2.34E⁻4
Character:	'H', '*', '□'

PASCAL

Standard Variable Type	Examples
INTEGER:	124, 10001, -102, +576
REAL:	1.276, -1027., 1.276E-14
BOOLEAN:	TRUE, FALSE
CHARACTER:	'A', '9'

Literals and constants have types but since their type can be determined by the compiler, we do not have to declare it.

COBOL

Type	Examples
Numeric Literal:	100.0, 25.32, 125
Non-numeric Literal:	"DEPRECIATION SCHEDULE" "12%"
Figurative Constants:	ZERO, SPACE, HIGH-VALUE, ALL

ALGOL-60

Type	Examples
Real:	2.102, 15.2E12 or 15E12
Integer:	-2117, 10, 1
Boolean:	TRUE, FALSE
String:	"$1235.50 EACH"

C

There are only a few basic data types in C:

char: a single byte, capable of holding one character in the local character set.

int: an integer, typically reflecting the natural size of integers on the host machine.

float: single-precision floating point.

double: double-precision floating point.

In addition, there are a number of qualifiers which can be applied to integers: short, long and unsigned. Short and long refer to different sizes of integers. Unsigned numbers obey the laws of arithmetic modulus 2^n, where n is the number of bits in an integer; unsigned numbers are always positive.

The declarations for the qualifiers look like:

```
short int x;
long int y;
unsigned int z;
```

The word 'int' can be omitted in such situations.

Type	Examples
int	124, 555, 576
float	137.8, 148.9, 0.12E3
double	123.456 e-7

(the "e" notion serves for both float and double)

char	'A', '9'

sizes of the objects are machine-dependent.

4. IDENTIFIERS

BASIC

BASIC identifiers are names denoting variables and constants. Numeric variable identifiers may be a letter, or a letter followed by a digit. String variable identifiers consist of a letter followed by a dollar sign, or a letter-digit-dollar sign.

Examples

Numeric: J, N, Y, C2
String: A1$, B$, X$

FORTRAN

FORTRAN identifiers are names denoting constants, variables, functions or subroutines. They must begin with a letter, which may be followed by any combination of letters and digits, with a maximum length of 6 characters. Identifiers of variables beginning with I, J, K, L, M, or N have the implicit data type INTEGER, others have an implicit data type REAL Other identifier types must be explicitly declared.

PL/1

PL/1 identifiers are names denoting constants, problem variables (arithmetic or string quantities), and program-control variables (labels, areas, offsets, pointer, event, task and priority variables). They can be up to 31 characters and must begin with a letter. Problem variables beginning with I, J, K, L, M or N implicitly represent binary, fixed point, real quantities; other variables implicitly represent decimal, floating point, real quantities. All variables can be explicitly declared for type. (See 6 below)

Examples

A, X123, CALC, ITEM

APL

An identifier may name a simple variable, an array, or a subprogram. After the first character, a name may consist of any combination of letters or digits. A name must not contain any embedded spaces. A name may be of any length. Only the first 77 characters are significant for variables and functions and only the first 11 characters are significant for workspaces. Characters in a name in excess of 77 are ignored.

Examples

AB32, WAD, ΔW235

PASCAL

Pascal identifiers are names denoting constants, variables, procedures and functions. They must begin with a letter, which may be followed by any combination and number of letters and digits. It may be of any length, but should differ from all other identifiers in the first eight characters for most computers. Further, none of the delimiter (reserved) words should be used as identifiers (See Appendix 1).

Examples

Pascal Delimiter
       Words: BEGIN, AND, IF, VAR

Programmer-defined
       Identifiers: A, CUSTOMER, A1B2, NUMBER

COBOL

COBOL identifiers are names denoting constants, variables and files. They can be up to 30 characters long and may include letters, digits and embedded hyphens. At least one character should be a letter. There are approximately 300 reserved words that cannot be used as identifiers (See Appendix II).

Examples

Reserved Words:

COBOL, INDEX, MOVE, END, SET

Programmer-defined identifiers:

HOURS, ENDING-INVENTORY, PREMIUM, A527157, 31576X5

ALGOL-60

ALGOL-60 identifiers are names denoting constants, variables, procedures and functions. They must begin with a letter, which may be followed by any combination of letters and digits, with a maximum length of 64 characters. Blanks can not appear. Variable types must be declared explicitly.

Examples

V, NSTAR, V67

C

An identifier in C is a sequence of letters and digits: the first character must be a letter. The underscore, _, counts as a letter. Upper and lower case letters are different; traditional C practice is to use lower case for variable names and all uppercase for symbolic constants. No more than the first eight characters are significant, although more may be used.

Furthermore, keywords like if, else, int, float etc. are reserved: you can't use them as variable names. (They must be in lower case.)

Examples

ab2, x, A2, Y9

5. DECLARATIONS

BASIC

Declarations are not necessary, and need not appear in any sequence. The variable or the data type is implied in the variable name.

Examples

A = 50.6 implies A is a numeric variable
A$ = "50.6" implies A$ is a string variable.

FORTRAN

Explicit declaration of variables is done with the INTEGER, REAL, DOUBLE PRECISION, COMPLEX, LOGICAL and EXTERNAL statements.

Examples

INTEGER	A,CMAX, T
REAL	J, NMAX, LIST, D(5)
COMPLEX	X1, X2, G(10,20)
LOGICAL	L, M, N

The variable names may be from one to six alphanumeric characters in length. EXTERNAL specifies that the names listed are subprogram names to be used as arguments in a call to a subroutine or function subroutine. The type declaration statements override the alphabetic naming convention of variables.

PL/1

Declaration of variables is through a DECLARE statement. Undeclared variables which begin with I, J, K, L, M, and N are assumed to be REAL, FIXED, BINARY and variables which begin with other letters are assumed to be REAL, FLOAT, DECIMAL.

Examples

DECLARE X REAL FLOAT DECIMAL;
DECLARE SUM REAL FIXED DECIMAL(8);
DECLARE A CHARACTER(40);

APL

Declarations for data are not necessary in APL. Indentifiers are not declared explicitly unless they are formal parameters or local identifiers in a subprogram (in which case the declaration serves only to indicate a scope of definition).

PASCAL

Declaration is accomplished in the data definition section for all identifiers (constants, labels, types and variables). This section may or may not contain any declarations (LABEL, CONST, TYPE, VAR).

Examples

```
LABEL     123;
CONST     SIZE=10;       (*integer valued*)
          FLOAT=5.3;     (*real valued*)
          LETTER='A';    (*character valued*)
TYPE      NUMBERS=INTEGER;
VAR       I,J  : NUMBERS;
          SUM  : REAL;
          A,B  : CHAR;
```

COBOL

Declaration of identifiers is in the DATA DIVISION.

Examples

```
01  CUSTOMER-RECORD.
    02  NAME PICTURE X(12).
    02  AMOUNT-DUE PICTURE  9999V99.
88  DAILY-RATE IS 50.0.
```

ALGOL-60

Declaration is accomplished with the BOOLEAN, INTEGER, REAL and STRING statements. Undeclared variables are assumed to be real.

Examples

```
REAL      V, JMIN;
INTEGER   V67, NSTAR;
BOOLEAN   W,X,Y;
```

C

All variables must be declared before use, although certain declarations can be made implicitly by context. A declaration specifies a type, and is followed by a list of one or more variables of that type.

1. Storage class specifiers:

   sc-specifier:
   auto
   static
   extern
   register
   typedef

The auto, static and register declarations also serve as definitions in that they cause an appropriate amount of storage to be reserved. In the extern case, there must be an external definition for the given identifiers somewhere outside the function in which they are declared.

(Continued on page 22)

5. DECLARATIONS

C

A register declaration is best thought of as an auto declaration, together with a hint to the compiler that the variables declared will be heavily used.

At most one sc-specifier may be given in a declaration. If the sc-specifier is missing from a declaration it is taken to be auto inside a function, extern outside.

Examples

(1) static char allocbuf [ALLOCSIZE];
        /*storage for alloc*/
(2) register FILE *iop;

2. Type specifiers:

> type-specifier:
>   char
>   short
>   int
>   long
>   unsigned
>   float
>   double

> struct- or union specifier
> typedef-name.

The words long, short, and unsigned may be thought of as adjectives; the following combinations are acceptable:

>   short int
>   long int
>   unsigned int
>   long float
> or
>   double

Here type int implies that the variables listed are integers; float stands for floating point, i.e., numbers which may have a fractional part. The sizes of these objects are machine-dependent.

3. Declarators:

The declarator-list appearing in a declaration is a comma-separated sequence of declarators, each of which may have an initializer.

C

> declarator-list:
>   init-declarator
>   init-declarator, declarator-list
> init-declarator:
>   declarator initializer$_{opt}$

The specifiers in the declaration indicate the type and storage class of the objects to which the declarators refer. Declarators have the syntax:

> declarator:
>   identifier
>   (declarator)
>   *declarator
>   declarator()
>   declarator [constant expression$_{opt}$]

Each declarator is taken to an assertion that when a construction of the same form as the declarator appears in an expression, it yields an object of the indicated type and storage class. Each declarator contains exactly one identifier, it is this identifier that is declared.

If an unadorned identifier appears as a declarator, then it has the type indicated by the specifier heading the declaration.

A declarator in parentheses is identical to the unadorned declarator, but the binding of complex declarators may be altered by parentheses.

Examples

In declaration TD_1, T is a type-specifier (like int etc.) and D_1 is a declarator. Suppose this declaration makes the identifier have type "...T," where "..." is empty if D_1 is just a plain identifier (so that type of x in "int x" is just int). Then if D_1 has the form

$$*D$$

the type of the contained identifier is "...pointer to T."

If D_1 has the form

$$D(\ )$$

then the contained identifier has the type "...function returning T."

If D_1 has the form

　　　D [constant-expression]

or

　　　　　D [ ]

then the contained identifier has type "...array of T."

　　　int i, *ip, f(), *fip(), (*pfi)();

The above declaration declares an integer i, a pointer ip to an integer, a function f returning an integer, a function fip returning a pointer to an integer, and a pointer pfi to a function which returns an integer.
The declaration

　　　float fa[17],　*afp[17];

declares an array of float numbers and an array of pointers to float numbers.

The declaration

　　　static int x3d [3][5][7];

declares a static three-dimensional array of integers, with rank 3X5X7.

4.　Structure and union declarations:

A structure is an object consisting of a sequence of named members. Each member may have any type. A union is an object which may, at a given time, contain any one of several members.

Structure and union specifiers have the same form:

　　struct-or-union-specifier:

　　　struct-or-union [struct-decl-list]
　　　struct-or-union identifier
　　　　　　　[struct-decl-list]
　　　struct-or-union identifier

　　struct-or-union:

　　　struct
　　　union

The struct-decl-list is a sequence of declarations for the members of the structure or union:

　　struct-decl-list:
　　　struct-declaration
　　　struct-declaration struct-decl-list
　　struct-declaration:
　　　type-specifier struct-declarator-list;
　　struct-declarator-list:
　　　struct-declarator
　　　struct-declarator, struct-declarator-list

A union may be thought of as a structure all of whose members begin at offset 0 and whose size is sufficient to contain any of its members. At most one of the members can be stored in a union at any time.

A structure or union specifier of the second form, that is, one of

　　　struct identifier [struct-decl-list]
　　　union identifier [struct-decl-list]

declares the identifier to be the structure tag (or union tag) of the structure specified by the list.

Example

Declaration of Structure

　　struct tnode [
　　　char fword [20];
　　　int count;
　　　struct tnode * left;
　　　struct tnode * right;
　　];

5.　Initialization:

A declarator may specify an initial value for the identifier being declared. The initializer is preceded by =, and consists of an expression or a list of values nested in braces.

(Continued on page 24)

5. DECLARATIONS

C

initializer:
    = expression
    = [initializer-list]
    = [initializer-list,]

Initializer-list can be an
    expression
    initializer-list, initializer-list
    [initializer-list]

<u>Examples</u>

(1) int x[] = {1,3,5};

declares and initializes x as a 1-dimensional array which has three members, since no size was specified and there are three initializers.

(2) float y[4][3] = {

            {1,3,5},
            {2,4,6},
            {3,5,7},

}; is a completely-bracketed initialization: 1,3 and 5 initialize the first row of the array y[0]; namely y[0] [0], y[0] [1], and y[0] [2]. Likewise,the next two lines initialize y[1] and y[2]. The initializer ends early and therefore y[3] is initialized to zero.

6. Type names:

In two contexts (to specify type conversions explicitly by means of a cast and as an argument 'of size of') it is desired to supply the name of a data type. This is accomplished using a "type name," which in essence is a declaration for an object of that type which omits the name of the object.

    type-name:
        type-specifier abstract -declarator
    abstract-declarator :
        empty
        (abstract-declarator)
        * abstract-declarator
        abstract-declarator ()
        abstract-declarator
                [constant-Expression$_{opt}$]

The named type is the same as the type of the

C

hypothetical identifier.

<u>Examples</u>

    int
    int*
    int*[3]
    int (*)[3]
    int * ()
    int (*) ()

name respectively the types "integer," "pointer to integer," "array of 3 pointers to integers," "function returning pointer to integer," and "pointer to function returning an integer."

7. Typedef:

Declarations whose "storage class" is typedef do not define storage, but instead define identifiers which can be used later as if they were type keywords naming fundamental or derived types.

    typedef-name:
        identifier

Within the scope of a declaration involving typedef, each identifier appearing as part of any declarator therein becomes syntactically equivalent to the type keyword naming the type associated with the identifier.

<u>Examples</u>

    typedef int   MILES, * KLICKSP;
    typedef struct   {double re,im;} complex;

the constructions

        MILES distance:
        extern KLICKSP metricp;
        complex z, *zp;

are all legal declarations.

The type of distance is int, that of metricp is "pointer to int," and that of z is the specified structure. ZP is a pointer to such a structure.

Typedef does not introduce brand new types, only synonyms for types which could be

C

specified in another way. Thus, in the example above, distance is considered to have exactly the same type as any other integer object.

6. ELEMENTARY STRUCTURED TYPE-ARRAY

BASIC

Arrays can be one or two dimensional. Rules for naming numeric and string arrays are the same as those for identifiers. Subscripts can range from 0 to 10 without declaration. Larger arrays must be declared. Array subscripts can be constants, variables, function references or expressions whose values must be integers. Non integer values are automatically truncated.

Examples

A(I),N(20),Y$(M),X(ABS(J(I))+5)

Arrays can be multidimensional in some advanced versions of BASIC.

FORTRAN

Arrays can be multidimensional. Rules for naming are same as those for identifiers. Size and type must be explicitly declared before use. Array subscripts can be constants, variables, function references or expressions whose values must be integers. Array elements are stored in memory with first subscript increasing more rapidly and last subscript least rapidly.

Examples

J(I),X(ABS(J(I))+5),LIST(13)
TABLE(4*I+2,K**3)

PL/1

Arrays can be multidimensional, with the same rules for naming as identifiers. Size and type must be explicitly declared before use. Array subscripts can be constants, variables, function references or expressions whose values must be integers. Non-integers are automatically truncated. Storage of array elements in memory is with last subscript increasing most rapidly and first subscript least rapidly. Usage of an asterisk instead of a subscript indicates all possible values of that subscript.

Examples

J(I),X(ABS(J(I))+5),LIST(13)
TABLE(4*I+2,*)

PL/1 has multidimensional heterogeneous arrays called structures which may be composed of variables, arrays or other structures organized in a hierarchical manner like COBOL.

APL

Multidimensional homogeneous arrays of either numbers or characters are the only structured data type. The array may have an arbitrary number of dimensions. The lower bound of the subscript range is implicitly 1 but may be set to 0 by a special command.

In standard APL, arrays of numeric or character data are homogeneous and can be scalar, vector, matrix, or higher order without any need to declare the shape or rank of the array. APL2 handles nested heterogeneous arrays (mixed or numeric and character as well as mixed rank).

PASCAL

Arrays can be multidimensional. Rules for naming arrays are same as those for identifiers. Each component or base type can be explicitly denoted and directly accessed by the name of the array followed by so called index in square brackets. Specification of component and index type is done in the data definition section. Index is any expression, which must yield a value in the range of the index type. The index type may be integer, boolean, character, enumeration or subrange, but not real.

Examples

A[I],N[20],YEAR[FEB]
MEM[I+J]

COBOL

COBOL arrays, called tables, can be one to three dimensional. Tables are named by the same rules as for identifiers. Tables must be defined in the DATA DIVISION. Subscripts may be numeric literals or data-names with positive integer values.

Examples

A(1),ELEM(7,21,3),MONTH(WHICH-ONE)

ALGOL-60

Arrays can be homogeneous and multidimensional. Rules for naming arrays are the same as rules for naming variables. Arrays may have an arbitrary number of dimensions with upper and lower bounds of each subscript range independently specified by the programmer. Thus, array sizes must be defined and type declaraed prior to use. The size of arrays may be made dependent on run-time data, so that storage for arrays cannot be allocated until run time.

Examples

V,T,LIST,TABLE

C

Arrays can be multidimensional. In C, array subscripts always start at zero instead of 1 as in FORTRAN or PL/1.

Examples

The declaration

        int ndigit [10];

declares ndigit to be an array of 10 integers. The elements are ndigit [0], ndigit [1]...... ndigit [9]. A subscript can be any integer expression, which of course includes integer variables like i and integer constants. C provides for retangular multidimensional arrays, although in practice they tend to be much less used than arrays of pointers.

7. ARRAY DECLARATION

BASIC

Arrays that need more than 10 storage locations must be declared in DIM(dimension) statement.

Examples

```
10  DIM V(100)
20  DIM M(10,20), N$(72)
```

The dimension statement DIM V(100) reserves 100 storage locations for the array V. Some advanced versions of BASIC have multidimensional arrays. The maximum number of dimensions for an array depends on the system and is often limited by the amount of memory available. The amount of space allocated for the elements of an array depends upon the type of array.

FORTRAN

Array sizes are usually declared with the DIMENSION statement. However, COMMON, COMPLEX, DOUBLE PRECISION, REAL, INTEGER, AND LOGICAL statements may also be used.

Examples

```
DIMENSION X(20), LIST(15), YEAR(25,25)
COMMON X(20), T(25,25)
DOUBLE PRECISION K(23)
```

PL/1

Sizes of arrays are declared with a DECLARE statement. The attributes of each array may follow each size declaration. If attributes are not specified and the initial character is I,J,K,L,M or N, then BINARY and FIXED are assumed. For all other cases DECIMAL FLOAT is assumed. The lower subscript bound is assumed to be 1, unless otherwise declared.

Examples

```
DECLARE J(10,20), K(10,20);
DECLARE TABLE(-1:N,M+1:200)
        DECIMAL FLOAT;
```

APL

Array declarations are not needed in APL.

PASCAL

Array component type and index type are specified in the data definition section. The general form of declaration is
$$A= \underline{ARRAY}[T1] \text{ OF } T2;$$
where A is an array, T1 is a scalar index type, and T2 is a component of any type.

Examples

VECTOR = ARRAY[1..N] OF REAL;
MATRIX = ARRAY[A..B,C..D] OF T;

COBOL

Tables are defined in the DATA DIVISION using the <u>OCCURS</u> clause.

Examples

```
01  THREE-DIM-ARRAY·
   02  PLANE OCCURS 20.
      03  ROW OCCURS 30.
         04  ELEM OCCURS 10 PIC 9999.
```

ALGOL-60

Array sizes are declared with the ARRAY statement, which may include the keywords BOOLEAN, INTEGER, OWN, REAL or STRING. An array is assumed to be real unless otherwise declared. Both upper and lower subscript bounds must be specified.

Examples

ARRAY A[1:25,1:35], B[1:20], C[1:50]
INTEGER ARRAY A[-10:20,3:N+2]
OWN Boolean Array B[1:20]
STRING ARRAY NAMES[1:100,1:5].

Note: Ordinarily, arrays are created on entry to the block in which they are declared and destroyed on exit from the block. But the optional <u>OWN</u> declaration however, allows retention of an array between block executions.

C

Array component type and index type are specified in the data definition section. The general form of declaration is TD1 where T is a type specifier and D is the declarative.

Examples

int ndigit[10];
char line[1000];
char *line ptr[LINES];

8. OPERATORS

BASIC

Arithmetic operators:

↑	Exponentiation	(1)
*	Multiplication	(2)
/	Division	(2)
+	Addition	(3)
−	Subtraction	(3)
=,<>,<,<=,>,>=;	Relational operators	
AND, OR, NOT;	Logical operators	

In the absence of parentheses, operations are performed according to the order of precedence from left to right.

FORTRAN

**	Exponentiation	(1)
*	Multiplication	(2)
/	Division	(2)
+	Addition	(3)
−	Subtraction	(3)
.EQ. .NE. .LT. .LE. .GT. .GE. }	Relationals	(4)
.NOT.	Logical NOT	(5)
.AND.	Logical AND	(6)
.OR.	Logical OR	(7)

In the absence of parentheses, operations are performed according to the order of precedence from left to right.

PL/1

**	Exponentiation	(1)
*	Multiplication	(2)
/	Division	(3)
+	Addition	(1 prefix, 3 infix)
−	Subtraction	(1 prefix, 3 infix)
‖ (or CAT)	Concatenation	(4)
=,¬=,<,<=,¬<,>,>=,¬> or =,NE,LT,LE, NL,GT,GE,NG	Comparisons	(5)
¬ (or NOT)	Bit-string NOT;	(1)
& (or AND)	Bit-string AND	(6)
| (or OR)	Bit-string OR	(7)
→ (or PT)	Pointer	

In the absence of parentheses, operations are performed in order of precedence from left to right, except when the operator is \|, in which case the precedence operations are carried out from right to left.

APL

In APL the order for arithmetic operations is from right to left. There is no hierarchy of operations; all operations take place in a right-to-left order. In APL and in ordinary mathematics, parentheses are used in the same way. They override the operation conventions and specify how the calculations should take place. In APL the sign of negation and the minus operation symbols are different.

Examples

1) $^-3 + 9 = 6$
2) $-3 + 9 = ^-12$

In example 1, the calculations move from right to left; 9 is added to a negative 3, giving an answer of positive 6. In Example 2, 9 is added to 3. This sum is then subtracted from zero, giving an answer of negative 12.

In APL, the asterisk symbol (*) indicates an exponentiation operation.

30

(Continued on Page 32)

8. OPERATORS

APL

Examples

```
2 * 3 = 8
2 * 3 + 2 * 0 = 16
2 * 3 + 5 * 2 = 268435456
```

Relational and Logical Operations:

In APL the Boolean values are represented by the numbers 1(true) and 0(false). The primitive relational operations are the usual 'equal', 'not equal', 'less-than', 'greater-than', 'less-than-or-equal to' and 'greater-than-or-equal to'. Logical operations include 'not', 'and', 'or', 'nand', and 'nor'. For details please see the table of APL operators.

Accessing:

Any variable may have an array as a value (or a single number or character). The entire array is retrieved just by referencing the variable in the usual way. However, individual array elements may also be accessed by subscripting.

Example

A[2;3] designates the element in the second row and the third column of the array A.

Subscripting is intended to allow arbitrary subarrays of an array to be accessed.

Example

A[;3] accesses the third column of the matrix A; Similarly, A[4;] gives the 4th row.

Three examples of APL operators are given below:

When applied to a vector in APL, reduction (symbol /) has the effect of placing a dyadic (i.e. two argument) operator between each element of the array.

Example

```
(1)  K ← 4 3 2 9
     +/K
     18
```

C

More interesting operators are the logical (connectives) && and ||. Expressions connected by &&(AND) or ||(OR) are evaluated left to right, and evaluation stops as soon as the truth or falsehood of the result is known.
The unary negation operator ! converts a non-zero or true operand into a 0, and a zero or false operand into a 1.

Increment and Decrement Operators:

C provides two unusual operators for incrementing and decrementing variables. The increment operator ++ adds 1 to its operand; the decrement operator -- subtracts 1. The unusual aspect is that ++ and -- may be used either as prefix operators (like ++n) or postfix operators (like n++).

Bitwise Logical Operators:

C provides a number of operators for bit manipulation; these may not be applied to float or double.

```
&    bitwise AND
|    bitwise inclusive OR
^    bitwise exclusive OR
<<   left shift
>>   right shift
~    one's complement(unary)
```

Example

(1) C = n & 0177:

Note that 0177(octal) is 000 001 111 111 in binary

Here bitwise AND operator '&' is used to mask off some set of bits. In the above example, it sets to zero all but low order 7 bits of n. The bitwise OR operator | is used to turn bits on:
x=x | MASK; sets to 'one' in X the bits that are set to 'one' in MASK.

You should carefully distinguish the bitwise operators, & and | from the logical connectives && and ||,which imply left to right evaluation of a truth value.

PASCAL

NOT	Logical NOT	(1)
*	Multiplication	(2)
/	Division	(2)
DIV	Integer division	(2)
MOD	Modular division	(2)
AND	Logical AND	(2)
+	Addition	(3)
-	Subtraction	(3)
OR	Logical OR	(3)
=,<>,<,<=,>,>,=	Relationals	(4)

In the absence of parentheses, operations are performed according to the order of precedence from left to right.

COBOL

	Unary minus/plus (multiplication by -1/+1)	(1)
**	Exponentiation	(2)
*	Multiplication	(3)
/	Division	(3)
+	Addition	(4)
-	Subtraction	(4)
=,<,>	Relationals	(5)
NOT	Logical Not	(6)
AND	Logical AND	(7)
OR	Logical OR	(8)

In the absence of parentheses, operations are performed according to the order of precedence from left to right. Keywords can be used instead of the above symbols except for **. A unique COBOL requirement is that all operators must have a space on each active side. For example, A-B is a name, not the subtraction of B from A, which requires A - B.

ALGOL-60

Exponentiation	↑ (or**)	(1)
Multiplication	*(or x)	(2)
Division {Real / Integer	/ ÷	(2)
Addition	+	(3)
Subtraction	-	(3)
Relational Primitives	=,≠,<,>,<=,>=	(4)
Boolean Primitives are		
NOT	⌐	(5)
AND	∧	(6)
OR	∨	(7)
IMP (implication)	⊃	(8)
EQV (equivalence)	≡	(9)

Operations within a hierarchical group are carried out from left to right.

C

The binary arithmetic operators are +,-,*,/, and the modulus operator is %. There is a unary -, but not unary +. The + and - operators have the same precedence, which is lower than the (identical) precedence of *, /, and %, which in turn are lower than unary minus. Arithmetic operators group left to right. Integer division truncates any fractional part. The expression x % y provides the remainder when X is divided by Y, and thus is zero when Y divides X exactly. The operator % can not be applied to float or double.

The relational operators are:

> >, >=, <, <=

They all have the same precedence. Just below them in precedence are the equality operators:

> ==(equal to), !=(not equal to)

which have the same precededence. Relational operators have lower precedence than arithmetic operators.

(Continued on page 32)

Example

(1) if x is 1 and y is 2, then x & y is zero while x && y is one.

The shift operators ≪ and ≫ perform left and right shifts of their left operand by the number of bit positions given by the right operand. Thus x≪2 shifts x left by two positions, filling vacated bits with 0; this is equivalent to multiplication by 4. Right shifting an unsigned quantity fills vacated bits with 0.

The unary operator ~ yields the one's complement of an integer; that is, it converts each 1-bit into a 0-bit and vice versa.

Example

Expression x &~007 masks the last six bits of x to zero.
    Since ~ 007 is ~ (000 111 111) = 111 000 000.

Assignment operators:

Most binary operators have a corresponding assignment operator op =, where op is one of the following:

$$+,-,*,/,\%,<<,\&,>>,|,\wedge$$

Example

The expression i = i+2 can be written in the compressed form i+=2

The conditional expression written with the ternary operator "?:" provides an alternate way to write the similar expression construction.

Example

```
(1)  if  (a>b)
         z=a;
     else
         z=b;
can be written as
z=(a>b) ? a:b;  / * z=max(a,b)  */
```

In general, consider the expression:
    e1 ? e2 : e3
In the above expression, e1 is evaluated first. If it is non-zero (true), then the expression e2 is evaluated, and that is the value of the conditional expression. Otherwise e3 is evaluated. C has no exponentiation operator.

Precedence and Order of Operation of Operators

Operator	Associativity	
(),[],→,·	Left to right	(1)
!,~,++,--,-,(type),*,& size of	right to left	(2)
*,/,%	left to right	(3)
+,-	left to right	(4)
<<,>>	left to right	(5)
<,<=,>,>=	left to right	(6)
==,!=	left to right	(7)
&	left to right	(8)
^	left to right	(9)
|	left to right	(10)
&&	left to right	(11)
||	left to right	(12)
?:	right to left	(13)
=,+=,-=,etc	right to left	(14)
,	left to right	(15)

8. OPERATORS

APL

```
(2)   R ← 2 3 2 1
      +/R (means 2+3+2+1 or 8).
   8
      x/R
  12
      */R
 512.
```

Two other generator primitives are inner product (symbol .) and outer product (symbol ∘). The inner product primitive takes two binary primitive operations and two arrays as arguments. The second primitive is applied to corresponding pairs of elements of the two arrays and then the first primitive is applied to reduce the result.

Example

Expression A+.xB, where A and B are vectors of the same length is equivalent to the expression +/(AxB), i.e., corresponding elements of A and B are multiplied to produce a new vector of the same length and then the elements of this new vector are added to produce a single number.

Other uses for the inner product primitive abound: for example, two vectors may be tested for component-by-component equality by the expression A+.≠B, which evaluates to zero only if A and B are identical.

The outer product function takes two arrays and a binary primitive as arguments and applies the primitive to each pair of elements of the two arrays, generating a new array whose number of dimensions is equal to the sum of the number of dimensions of the two original arrays. Thus, the outer product of two vectors results in the creation of a matrix, the outer product of a vector and a matrix gives an array of three dimensions, etc.

On some APL systems, such as IBM APL2, it is possible to create user-defined operators. (See Appendix VII for a list of APL operators).

9. EXPRESSIONS

BASIC

BASIC expressions are constructed using infix notation. Numerical quantities are represented by arithmetic expressions, while Boolean quantities are represented by logical expresions.

Examples

Arithmetic expressions:
x * y, J/2, SIN(x), A↑2+B↑2
Boolean expressions:
P >=Q
A <>B

FORTRAN

FORTRAN expressions are constructed using infix notation. Numerical quantities are represented by arithmetic expressions, while Boolean quantities are represented by logical or Boolean expressions.

Examples

Arithmetic expressions:
X*Y, J/2, SIN(X), A**2+B**2
Boolean expressions:
P.GE.Q
(P.EQ.Q) AND (A.EQ.B)

PL/1

PL/1 expressions are constructed using infix notation. They can be element (scalar) expressions which refer to single items of data or array and structure expressions which refer to arrays and structures. Expressions may be further classified as arithmetic, relational, bit-string or concatenation.

Examples

Arithmetic:
x * y, J/2, A**2+B**2
Relational:
P >=Q
(P=Q) & (A >=B)
Bit-string:
K & '0100'B
A/C
Concatenation:
NAME//ADDRESS
x//'ABC'

APL

APL operations appear only in two forms, regardless of whether they are primitives or programmer-defined subprograms.
1. Binary operations (operations with two operands) are written in infix notation.

Examples
A-B

2. Unary operations (operations with one operand) are written in reverse polish notation.

Example
-C

The only exception to this rule is the subscripting operation, which is represented

(Continued on Page 38)

PASCAL

PASCAL expressions are constructed by observing two important features of PASCAL: (1) the grammar of expression which is the familiar infix notation, (2) the type of data. The type of data affects the kinds of operators allowed in the expression. For example, integer data cannot be modified by real operator without first being converted to reals.

Examples

Integer expressions:
J DIV 2, X+J, (J+1)MOD(J-1)
Real expressions:
X * Y, J/2, SIN(x)
Boolean expressions:
P OR Q, P AND Q, (P ORQ) and (A=B)
S<>R
Character expression:
ORD(C)-ORD('A')
Set expressions:
A-['0' .. '9'] ['A','B']<=['A','B','C']

COBOL

COBOL has arithmetic and Boolean expressions. Arithmetic expressions are used in the COMPUTE verb format. At least one space must separate each operator symbol from the preceding and following data-names.

Examples

Arithmetic expressions:

X * Y, J / 2, (A ** 2 + B ** 2)

Boolean expressions:

PNOT<Q   or   P NOT LESS THAN Q
(P=Q) AND (A NOT EQUAL TO B)

ALGOL-60

ALGOL-60 expressions are constructed using infix notation. Arithmetic expressions represent numerical quantities.

Example

SQRT((BASE↑2) + HEIGHT ↑2)

Boolean expressions represent conditions which are either true or false.

Example

P=Q
(P=Q) · (A=B)
A<=C

C

C expressions are constructed using infix notation. Numerical quantities are represented by arithmetic expressions, while Boolean quantities are represented by logical expressions.

Examples

(1) Arithmetic expressions:
    x*y, x%y, x+y
(2) Boolean expressions:
    x>=y
    x!=z
(3) Assignment expressions:
    i=i+3
or i +=3
    x=x*(y+1)
or x*=y+1

9. EXPRESSIONS

by enclosing the subscript in a pair of brackets. eg. D[4].

An APL expression is always evaluated from right to left with the operands of an operation evaluated before the operation is applied.

Example

A-B+C+D is evaluated as A-(B+(C+D)).
2x3+5*2 is evaluated as 2x(3+(5*2)).

Note that the right-to-left rule applies to programmer-defined function subprograms as well as built-in primitives. Since no special syntax is provided for function subprogram calls, they also appear as infix operations.

For example:
A FUN B represents the function call FUN(A,B). A-B FUN C÷D is evaluated as A-(B FUN(C÷D)) or A-FUN (B,(C÷D)).
Any expression may include the ☐ (quad) operation specifying a request for numeric input from the programmer's terminal.

10. ASSIGNMENT

BASIC

Assignment is achieved with the LET statement or with a combination of READ and DATA statements.

Examples

```
LET A = 145.27
LET X2$ = "WADOOD"
READ T    ⎫  500 will be assigned to the
DATA 500  ⎭  variable T.
```

LET in the above statements is optional.

FORTRAN

Assignment is achieved with assignment statements and DATA statements.

Examples

```
HYPO = SQRT((BASE**2) + HEIGHT**2)
ISUM = ISUM +1
DATA x,y,z, / 1.717, 3.546E2, -5.2/
DATA ICHF, ICHC/'F','C'/
```

Note the difference between this data statement and the data statement used in BASIC. In this case, 1.717 is assigned to x, 3.546E2 is assigned to y and so on.

PL/1

Assignment is achieved by the assignment statement. Single variables, multiple variables, arrays or structures can all be assigned values by an assignment statement.

Examples

```
HYPO=SQRT((BASE**2)+HEIGHT**2);
SUM=SUM+1;
X,Y,Z=1.717;
K(2),X,Z=2*Q
NAME='STEVE COWE';
X,Y=P+Q; (where arrays are identical in
             dimension and subscript range)
```

APL

A single value (a scalar), or several values (a vector), can be assigned to a variable and stored in a workspace. This operation is accomplished by printing a variable, a left-pointing arrow and the scalar or vector to be stored.

Example

$$A \leftarrow 15.3$$

The scalar 15.3 is assigned to the variable A. Vectors can be assigned to variables in exactly the same way

$$V \leftarrow 3\ 6\ 9\ 12\ 15$$

Refer to Section 15 (LIBRARY FUNCTIONS) for an example of how higher order arrays are created and assigned.

PASCAL

Assignment is achieved with the assignment statements.

Examples

```
J:=(J+1)MOD(J-1);
HYPO:=SQRT(SQR(BASE)+SQR(HEIGHT));
FLAG:=TRUE;
A:=['A'..'Z','0'..'9'];
```

COBOL

Assignment is achieved in the DATA DIVISION entries using the VALUE clause along with the PICTURE clause or using appropriate PROCEDURE DIVISION statements.

Examples

DATA DIVISION statements:

```
01 END-OF-DATA  PICTURE 9 VALUE ZERO.
02 FILLER          PICTURE X(4) VALUE 'WEEK'.
```

PROCEDURE DIVISION statements:

```
MOVE ZERO TO WEEK-COUNTER
ADD  W,X   TO Y
SUBTRACT Y,Z FROM X
MULTIPLY Y BY Z
COMPUTE A = A + B * C / D ** 2
READ IN-FILE AT END MOVE 1 TO EOF-FLAG.
```

ALGOL-60

Assignment is achieved with assignment statements. It allows multiple variable assignment.

Examples

```
HYPO:=SQRT(SQR(BASE) + SQR(HEIGHT));
A:=B:=C:=4;
A:=A+1;
```

C

Assignment is achieved with the assignment statements.

Example

```
celsius =(5.0/9.0) * (fahr-32.0);
    i = i*4
or
    i * =4.
```

11. CONDITIONAL AND UNCONDITIONAL BRANCHING

BASIC

Unconditional branching is achieved by GOTO and GOSUB statements.
```
     Examples: GOTO  200
               GOSUB  1000
```
Every GOSUB must have a RETURN statement.

In BASIC, conditional branching is achieved by using IF.....THEN and ON.....GOTO statements. These two statements coupled with the unconditional GOTO statement can be used to simulate the IF.....THEN......ELSE statement as shown in the example below.

Examples

Simulated IF-THEN-ELSE construct:
```
140  IF K>=10 THEN 190
150  REM ELSE
160  LET B=B+C
170  LET K=K+1
180  GOTO 210
190  REM THEN
200  LET B=B/10
210  STOP
```

Simulated CASE construct:
```
 90  ON K GOTO 100, 130, 160
100  REM PERIMETER OF RECTANGLE
110  LET P=2*(H+W)
120  GOTO 190
130  REM PERIMETER OF CIRCLE
140  LET P=2*3.14*R
150  GOTO 190
160  REM PERIMETER OF TRIANGLE
170  LET P=S1+S2+SQR(S1↑2+S2↑2-2*S1*S2*COS(A))
180  GOTO 190
190  STOP.
```

FORTRAN

Unconditional branching is achieved by the GO TO statement. The general form of the GO TO statement is GO TO n where n is a statement number.

Example

```
      I=1
      AB=0
20    AB=AB+I
      GO TO 20
```

In FORTRAN, conditional branching is achieved by using combinations of arithmetic IF, logical IF, computed GO TO and GO TO statements. In the arithmetic IF statement, the basis of selection is based on whether the arithmetic value of the specified arithmetic expression is less than, equal to or greater than zero.

Examples

Arithmetic IF statement:
    FORMAT: IF expression n_1, n_2, n_3

where expression is a fixed point or floating point arithmetic expression and n_1, n_2, n_3 are statement numbers. First the value of the expression is evaluated and depending upon its value, the control is transferred. If 'a' is an expression, then control is transferred to n_1 n_2 or n_3, depending on whether $a<0$, $a = 0$ or $a > 0$ respectively.

    Example: IF (X-100) 10,10,20

Logical IF statement:
    FORMAT: IF exp s

Here, exp is a logical expression and s is any executable FORTRAN statement other than a DO statement or any other logical IF statement. IF exp is true, s is executed, else program execution proceeds to the next statement.

Examples

```
IF (X.LE.100.) GO TO 200
IF (A.GT.B)  X=X+1
IF (.NOT.(X)) GO TO  100
```

(Continued on Page 46)

PASCAL

Unconditional branching is achieved by the GOTO statement. In PASCAL, this statement is not a very useful statement because programs can be written without it. The general form of a GOTO statement is GOTO n where n is a statement label. The label used in a GOTO statement must be declared and it has to be a positive integer.

Example

```
Procedure donut;
LABEL 5;
BEGIN
......
5:....
......
GOTO 5;
END;
```

In Pascal, conditional branching is achieved by using IF-THEN-ELSE and CASE constructs. Nesting is possible.

Examples

IF-THEN-ELSE construct:

```
IF COUNT < 10 THEN
  BEGIN
    CBAL:=CBAL+CCHG;
    COUNT:=COUNT+1
  END
ELSE
    CBAL:=CBAL/10;
```

CASE construct:

```
CASE KIND OF
    RECT: PERIMETER:=2*(HEIGHT+WIDTH);

    CIRC: PERIMETER:=2*PI*RADIUS;
    TRI:  PERIMETER:=SIDE1+SIDE2
            +SQRT(SQR(SIDE1)+SQR(SIDE2)
            -2*SIDE1*SIDE2*COS(ANGLE))
    END
```

This example shows that the case statement is a generalization of the IF....THEN statement. In this example, it replaces three IF....THEN statements.

COBOL

Unconditional branching is achieved in PROCEDURE DIVISION with GO TO-procedure-name statement.

Examples

GO TO SALARY-COMP

GO TO REPEAT

In COBOL, conditional branching is achieved using IF-ELSE and GO TO (with DEPENDING clause) constructs. Nesting is possible.

Examples

IF-ELSE construct :

```
IF COUNT IS LESS THAN 10.0

    ADD CCHG TO CBAL
    ADD 1 TO COUNT
ELSE
    DIVIDE 10 INTO COUNT.
```

Simulated CASE construct:

```
    GO TO CASE1,CASE2,CASE3  DEPENDING

        ON KIND.
    .
    .
CASE1.
    .
    .
    GO TO END-CASE.
CASE2.
    .
    .
    GO TO END-CASE.
CASE3.
    .
    .
    GO TO END-CASE.
END-CASE.
    EXIT.
```

(See Remaining Languages on Following Page)   43

11. CONDITIONAL AND UNCONDITIONAL BRANCHING

PL/1

Unconditional branching is achieved by the GOTO statement. The general format of the GOTO statement is GOTO ℓ , where ℓ is a statement label. The statement branched to must have at least one label preceding it and must not be a procedure statement.

Example

REP: A = B+C
.
.
.
.
    GOTO REP;

Conditional branching is achieved by the
IF....THEN.... and
IF....THEN....ELSE....statements.

Examples

FAST: TEMP = LAST+F;
         N = N+1
         IF N < 15 THEN GOTO REPEAT;
         END PROCEDURE

S1: IF #_SHPG < 31
     THEN S2: IF #_SHPG > 0
               THEN AVGE_$=TOTAL/#_SHPG
     ELSE GOTO ERROR_#;

Unconditional branching is accomplished by means of a GOTO statement label construct.

Example

GOTO START;
GOTO 15;
GOTO 15;

The basic **GOTO** control transfer is augmented by an additional feature. A switch, in its simplest form, is simply a vector of statement labels. A switch declaration at the beginning of a block specifies the sequence of labels the switch contains. For example, the declaration switch $S:=L_1,L_2,SY,NEXT$ at the beginning of a block sets up a vector S containing the four statement labels $L_1,L_2,SY,NEXT$. Within

APL

Branching in APL uses the right arrow ($\rightarrow$). There are many different methods of branching but most experienced programmers prefer the following:

Conditional branch

$$\rightarrow condition/Label$$

Without detailing how the 'reduction' operate (/) works, the above statement gives a branch to a line denoted 'label' if 'condition' is true (logical 1), OR execution will continue to the next program line if false (logical 0).

Multi-way conditional branch

$$\rightarrow(Cond1, Cond2, Cond3)/Label1,Label2, Label3$$

The above statement branches to one of several lines depending on which condition is evaluated as true.

Unconditional branch

$$\rightarrow Label$$
$$or$$
$$\rightarrow Line\ number$$

Branches can be made to designated line numbers (e.g. $\rightarrow$ 5 would branch to line [5]) but this is bad programming practice since line numbers are dynamically relocated whenever a program change is made.

(Continued on Page 46)

ALGOL-60

In ALGOL-60 conditional branching is achieved by using an IF-THEN-ELSE statement and a designational expression. A designational expression is an expression whose value is a statement label. Designational expression may be constructed only from statement labels, switch references and IF...THEN...ELSE conditional branching structures.

Examples

IF X=Y THEN GO TO START;
IF X<=Y THEN GO TO DIV1 ELSE GO TO DIV2;

Nested IF-THEN-ELSE statement:
IF X>=Y THEN GO TO START ELSE
IF Z<=A THEN GO TO FINISH ELSE X:=X+1;

GO TO statement with designational expression:
GO TO if X=Y then L_1 else if X>Y then L_2 else L_3;
switch S: = L_1, if X=Y then L_2 else L_3, SY,NEXT
is a valid switch declaration. A subsequent GO TO S[2] causes a transfer to statement L_2 or L_3 depending on whether X=Y or X≠Y.

C

Unconditional branching: Control may be transferred unconditionally by means of the statement

go to identifier;

The identifier must be a label located in the current function.

Example

go to start;

start:........

In C, conditional branching is achieved using IF-ELSE, ELSE-IF and SWITCH constructs. Nesting is possible.

Examples

IF-ELSE construct :
```
    if (n >0) {
       if (a >b)
          z=a;
        }
       else
          z=b;
```

ELSE-IF construct :
```
    if (i >0) {
       if (x> y)
           T=x+1;
       else if (x< y)
          s=x-1;
        }
       else
          T=y;
```

Switch construct:

The switch statement is a special multi-way decision maker that tests whether an expression matches one of the numbers of constant value and branches accordingly.

Example

```
while ((c=getchar()) !=EOF)
    switch (c) {
         case '0':
         case '1':
         case '2':
```

(Continued on Page 47)

11. CONDITIONAL AND UNCONDITIONAL BRANCHING

FORTRAN

Computed GO TO statement:

$$\text{FORMAT: GO TO}(n_1, n_2, n_3, \ldots n_m), I$$

where $n_1, n_2, \ldots n_m$ are statement numbers and I is a fixed point variable such that $1 \leq I \leq m$. This statement is used to transfer control to a program statement depending upon the value of I. If I=1, the control is transferred to n_1; if I=2 the control is transferred to n_2 and so on.

Examples

GO TO (10, 5,28,15), L
GO TO (150, 100, 200, 10), M4

Assigned GO TO statement:

$$\text{FORMAT: GO TO R}, (S_1, S_2, \ldots S_n)$$

where R is an unsigned fixed point variable appearing in a previously executed ASSIGN statement and $S_1, S_2, \ldots S_n$ are statement numbers. The assigned GO TO statement causes the statement with the statement number equal to the value of R that was last assigned by an ASSIGN statement.

Examples

GO TO   J, (40,30,20)
GO TO   FM, (100,800,1000)

PL/1

the block, a GOTO of the form GOTOS[2] may be used to transfer control to statement L_2. Thus, a switch serves simply as a technique for programming an unconditional multiway branch.

```
    case '3':
    case '4':
    case '5':
    case '6':
    case '7':
    case '8':
    case '9':
          ndigit[c-'0'] ++;
       break;
    default:
       nother ++;
       break;
    }
```

Here the switch evaluates the character c and compares its value to all the cases. Each case must be labeled by an integer, character constant or constant expression. If a case matches the expression value, execution starts at that case. The case labeled default is executed if none of the other cases is satisfied.

The break statement causes an immediate exit from the switch.

12. LOOPING/ITERATION

BASIC

In BASIC, looping or iteration is achieved by the combination of FOR..... and NEXT..... statements. The FOR.....NEXT..... statements can be nested.

Example

```
10    For I = 1 TO 10
20      READ A
30      LET B=B+A
40      PRINT B
50    NEXT I
```

Note that the initial value of B is 0. If a variable appears in a program for the first time, then a zero is assigned to it.

FORTRAN

FORTRAN loops are achieved using a DO statement in the beginning and a numbered executable statement at the end. Loops can be nested.

Examples

Simple loop:

```
         DO 70 I=1,N
           .
           .
           .
70       CONTINUE
```

Simulated DO-WHILE construct:

```
700    IF(I.GE.N) GO TO 780
         .
         .
         .
       GO TO 700
780    CONTINUE
```

Simulated REPEAT-UNTIL construct:

```
800    CONTINUE
       I=I + 1
         .
         .
         .
880    IF(I.NE.N) GO TO 800
```

PL/1

In PL/1 we have a basic DO construct for iteration or looping. The construct must begin with a DO statement and end with an END statement. Loops can be nested.

APL

Looping in APL is achieved with conditional or unconditional branches. The following demonstrates how a loop can be written in APL:

 (Continued on Page 50)   (Continued on Page 50)

PASCAL

In Pascal there are three forms of loop constructs to choose from: FOR, WHILE and REPEAT. All choice constructs and looping constructs can be nested within each other.

Examples

Simple loop:

```
FOR I:=1 TO N DO
    BEGIN
        .
        .
        .
    END
```

DO-WHILE construct:

```
WHILE I< N DO
    BEGIN
        .
        .
        .
    END
```

REPEAT-UNTIL construct:

```
REPEAT
    I:=I+1;
        .
        .
        .
UNTIL I=N;
```

COBOL

COBOL achieves iteration of paragraphs or sections by means of the perform statements in the PROCEDURE DIVISION.

Examples

Simple loop:

```
PERFORM PAR1 VARYING COUNTER
        FROM 1 BY 1
        UNTIL COUNTER EQUAL TO 20.
```

Simulated DO-WHILE construct:

```
PERFORM PAR1
        UNTIL COUNTER NOT<20.
    .
    .
    .
PAR1.
    .
    .
    ADD 1 TO COUNTER.
```

Simulated REPEAT-UNTIL construct:

```
PERFORM PARA-1.
PERFORM PARA-1 UNTIL I = N.
    .
    .
    .
PARA-1.
    ADD 1 TO I.
```

ALGOL-60

In ALGOL-60 loops are achieved using FOR-DO pair of statements. A loop consists of a simple or a compound statement. The FOR statement takes one of the following forms:

```
for <variable> : = <List of values >do < body >
for<variable>: =<expr >while<Boolean expr >
do< body>
```

C

In C there are three forms of loop constructs to choose from: FOR, WHILE and DO. All choice and looping constructs can be nested.

(Continued on Page 51)

(Continued on Page 51)

12. LOOPING/ITERATION

<table>
<tr><td align="center">**PL/1**</td><td align="center">**APL**</td></tr>
</table>

Examples

Simple loop:

```
{   DO I = 1 TO N;
    .
    .
    .
    END;
```

DO-WHILE construct:

```
{   DO WHILE (I < N);
    .
    .
    .
    END;
```

Simulated REPEAT-UNTIL construct:

```
{   I = I + 1;
    DO WHILE (I ~= N);
    I = I +1;
    .
    .
    .
    END;
```

```
    ∇ FAC J
[1] Z←I←1
[2] LOOP:→(I≥J)/RESULT
[3] I←I+1 ◊ Z←Z×I
[4] →LOOP
[5] RESULT ; Z
[6]∇
```

The above function computes the factorial of a number J. The loop in this function consists of the statements on lines [2], [3], and [4]. The unconditional branch to label 'loop' in Line [4] causes the statements on these lines to be executed until the conditional statement in line [2] (i.e. $I \geq J$) evaluates to logical 1. When this occurs, a branch is made to label 'RESULT' (i.e. line [5]). The value of the factorial of J which has been stored in the variable Z is then output. (Note: This function has been written to illustrate how a loop can be coded in APL. The APL primitive function '!' should be used when computing factorials).

A major feature of APL which sets it apart from many other languages is its ability to avoid explicit looping in many cases. Examples of how many types of loop can be avoided:

a) +/'F' = TEXTSTRING

The above statement returns a count of all occurrences of the letter 'F' in the vector 'TEXTSTRING'.

Example: The statement,

+/'r' = 'Brontosaurus Burgers'

will return the value of 4.

b.) V←((M+ιl+N-M)-1)*2

The above statement will return a vector, V, consisting of the squares of the integers from M to N inclusive.

c.) SUMSQ←+/V

The above statement returns a scalar, SUMSQ, which contains the sum of the squares which are contained in the vector, V, of example (b).

ALGOL-60

for < variable > : =< init-val > step< incr-val >
until< final-val>do <body>

Simple loop:

```
FOR I : = 2,3,5,7,11,13  do BEGIN...END;
FOR Q : = 1 step 1 until 25 do BEGIN...END;
```

Conditional loop:

```
FOR K : = K+1 while K<N∧X>0 do BEGIN...END;
```

Nested loop:

```
FOR R : = 1 STEP 1 UNTIL S DO
FOR T : = 1 STEP 1 UNTIL U DO

    B[R]:=B[R]+A[R,T]*X[T]
```

The three basic forms of FOR statement head
elements may be combined, as in
FOR I:= 2,3,7,11,15 step 1 Until 20, I+2 while
        I≤N∧X<0 do BEGIN....END.

C

Examples

(1)   while (x >0){
            T = y/x + c;
            M = x+c;
        }

In general, while (expression)
        statement
Here the expression is evaluated. If it is
non-zero, statement is executed and expression
is re-evaluated. This cycle continues until expression becomes zero, at which point execution
resumes after statement.

(2)   The for statement:

            for (expr1; expr2; expr3)
                statement
        is equivalent to
            expr1;
            while (expr2){
            statement
                expr3;
        }

Example

The following loop fills an array with integers
by calls to get int:
    int n,v, array[size];
for (n=0; n< size&&getint (&v) !=EOF; n ++)
    array[n]=v;
Here each call sets v to the next integer
found in the input.

(3)   Do-while construct:

The while and for loops share the desirable
attribute of testing the termination condition
at the   top.   The   third   loop in   C, the
do-while, tests at the bottom after making
each pass through the loop body; the body
is always executed at least once. The syntax
is   do
        statement
    while (expression):
The statement is executed, then expression is
evaluated. If it is true, statement is evaluated
again and so on. If the expression becomes
false, the loop terminates.

Example
    do   {
        M[i++] = n%10 + '0';
    }
    while ((n/=10) > 0);

13. FUNCTIONS (user defined)

BASIC

Single-line and multi-line functions can be defined in a BASIC program. All function declarations begin with a DEF statement. Multi-line functions end with a FNEND statement.

Examples

Function definition:
    20 DEF FNH(A,B) = SQR((B↑2) +H↑2)

Function reference:

    .
    .
    .

  60 LET Z=FNH(X,Y)

    .
    .
    .

Function definition:
```
 ⎧ 30  DEF FNI(M,Y,F,I)
 ⎪ 40  LET N=((M*1760+Y)*3+F)*12+I
 ⎨     .
 ⎪     .
 ⎪     .
 ⎩ 60  FNEND
```

Function reference:

    .
    .
    .

  100 LET L=FNI(A,B,C,D)

FORTRAN

A function whose value may be computed in a single arithmetic or logical expression may be defined as a statement function, local to a particular subprogram. Functions with more than one statement are compiled as separate subprograms, which begin with a FUNCTION statement and end with an END statement. One or more RETURN statements which have the effect of terminating execution of subprogram and returning to point of call in the main program may be included in the function subprogram at logical termination points.

Examples

Statement function definition:
    HYP(A,B)=SQRT(A**2+B**2)

Function reference:

    .
    .
    .

  Z=HYP(X,Y)

    .
    .
    .

Function declaration:
```
 ⎧ FUNCTION INCHES(M,Y,F,I)
 ⎪ INCHES=((M*1760+Y)*3+F)*12+I
 ⎪     .
 ⎨     .
 ⎪     .
 ⎪ RETURN
 ⎩ END
```

Function reference:

    .
    .
    .

  LENGTH=INCHES(A,B,C,D)

    .
    .
    .

PASCAL

Function declarations begin with the word FUNCTION. The type ·of the function and the parameters are specified in the heading of the declaration. The body of the function declaration is a block and may contain any set of statements. An assignment to the name of the function must be included in the block.

Example

Function declaration:
```
FUNCTION INCHES(M,Y,F,I:INTEGER):INTEGER;
BEGIN
INCHES:=((M*1760+Y)*3+F)*12+I
END;
```

Function reference:
```
      .
      .
      .
   LENGTH:=INCHES(A,B,C,D);
```

COBOL

Functions are not defined in COBOL.

(See Remaining Languages on Following Page)

13. FUNCTIONS (user defined)

PL/1

A procedure block is headed by a PROCEDURE statement and terminated by an END statement. Each procedure must have a name, that is, each PROCEDURE statement must be labeled. A procedure name denotes an entry point through which control can be transferred to the procedure. A procedure can be structured as a function if it returns a single value. This single value to be passed to the calling procedure is specified in the parentheses of a RETURN statement.

Example

Procedure definition:

```
    INCHES:PROCEDURE(M,Y,F,I);
    INCHES=((M*1760+Y)*3+F)*12+I;
    .
    .
    RETURN(INCHES);
    END;
```

Procedure Reference:

```
        .
        .
        .
        .
    . LENGTH=INCHES(A,B,C,D);
        .
        .
        .
        .
        .
```

APL

Functions in APL are classified on the basis of two main criteria:
(1) The number of arguments contained in the header.
(2) Whether the function is limited or unlimited.

A limited function has a restricted use. It produces an error condition when used in a compound expression or within another function, unless it is the last function to be executed.

An unlimited function can be used in any compound expression or within another function without causing an error condition.

Monadic function: A function containing one argument in its header is called monadic.

Example of an unlimited, monadic function.

```
            ∇S← SQUARE N
    [1]      S←N*2
    [2]      ∇
output:          SQUARE 25
            625
```

SQUARE is monadic because it contains one argument in its header. The argument is N. SQUARE is unlimited because it can be used effectively in APL expressions or in other APL functions.

Examples

```
            4 x 5 + SQUARE 5
output:   120
            ∇C ← CIRCLE R
    [1]     C ← o1 x SQUARE R
    [2]     ∇
            CIRCLE 7
output:     153.93791
```

Note: The APL primitive oy (Pi times) is used in line [1]. This function is equivalent to πy. Therefore, o1 is equivelent to π.

Here SQUARE is used within the function CIRCLE, which is also an unlimited, monadic function.

By contrast, a limited function is characterized by the absence of the left-pointing arrow and

(Continued on Page 56)

ALGOL-60

In ALGOL-60 a function can be constructed as a procedure which is a self-contained program segment beginning with a procedure statement and consisting of one or more statements and/or blocks.

Example

Procedure definition:
```
    REAL PROCEDURE CONST(A,B,P₁,Q₁);
    VALUE A,B,P₁,Q₁;
    REAL A,B,P₁,Q₁;
    BEGIN
    .
    .
    .
    CONST:=5+(P₁+Q₁)*(A+B);
    END;
```

Procedure Reference:
```
    .
    .
    .
    R:=T*CONST(A,B,4,P₁+Q₁);
    .
    .
    .
    .
```

C

In C, a function is equivalent to a subroutine or function in Fortran, or a procedure in PL/1, Pascal, etc. A function provides a convenient way to encapsulate some computation in a black box, which can then be used without worrying about its innards.

Example

Since C has no exponentiation operator like ** of Fortran or PL/1, then the mechanics of function definition by writing a function power (m,n) which raises an integer 'm' to a positive integer power 'n' are illustrated as follows.

```
    main()        /*test power function*/
    {
    int i;
    for (i=o; i<10; ++i)
      print f("%d %d %d\n", i,power(2,i),power
          (-3,i));
      }
    power(x,n)    /*raise x to n-th power; n>0*/
      int x,n;
        {
        int i, p;
        p=1
        for(i=1; i<=n; ++i)
           p=p*x;
        return(p);
        }
```

Each function has the same form:
```
    name(argument list, if any)
    argument declarations, if any
      {
          declarations
          statements
      }
```

In C, all function arguments are passed "by value". This means that the called function is given the values of its arguments in temporary variables(actually on a stack) rather than their addresses. The main distinction is that in C the called function cannot alter a variable in the calling function; it can only alter its private, temporary copy.

13. FUNCTIONS (user defined)

a storage variable that is contained in both the header and the body of the function.

Example

```
      ∇SQUARE 1 N
[1]   N*2
[2]   ∇
          SQUARE 1 5
      25
          3x6 + SQUARE 1 5
      25
   VALUE ERROR
          3x6 + SQUARE 1 5
                       ∧
```

From the above example it is clear that when SQUARE 1 is used within an arithmetic expression or within another function, it produces error conditions. SQUARE 1 is monadic because it contains one argument in its header. It is a limited function because it fails to return valid results when placed within an arithmetic expression or within another function.

Dyadic functions: Functions that contain two arguments in their headers are classified as dyadic.

Example

```
      ∇ R ← N  ROUNDOFF  D
[1]   M ← N+5x10 *⁻(D+1)
[2]   M ← ⌊Mx10*D
[3]   R ← Mx10*⁻D
[4]   ∇
          258.6567  ROUNDOFF  2
```

output: 258.66

Here the first argument, N, represents the number to be rounded. The second argument, D, denotes the number of places to which it is to be rounded. Thus ROUNDOFF is an unlimited function because the ←(assignment arrow) in both the header and the last statement of the body of the function store the result in R.

By contrast, a limited dyadic function is charaterized by the absence of a left pointing arrow and storage variable in both the header and the body of the function.

APL

```
      ∇R  CYLINDVOL  H
[1]   ' THE VOLUME OF THE CYLINDER IS:'
[2]   V←o1xHxR*2
[3]   V
[4]   ∇
```

output:
```
          7 CYLINDVOL 14
     THE  VOLUME  OF  THE  CYLINDER
  IS:

          2155.13074
```

Niladic functions; Functions that do not contain arguments in their headers are classified as niladic functions.

Example

```
      ∇ NETPAY
[1]   'ENTER HOURS'
[2]   H←□
[3]   'ENTER RATE'
[4]   R←□
[5]   G←HxR
[6]   →OVERTIME x ι (H>40)
[7]   P←G-Gx0.25
[8]   →PAY
[9]   OVERTIME:G←G+(H-40)xRx0.5
[10]  P←G-Gx0.25
[11]  PAY:'YOUR PAY IS'; P ROUNDOFF 2
[12]  ∇
```

output:
```
       NETPAY
  ENTER HOURS
  □:

       45
  ENTER RATE
  □:

       2.50
  YOUR PAY IS 89.06
```

Here the user-defined function ROUNDOFF is a subroutine.

14. SUBROUTINES

BASIC

A subroutine consists of a block of statements. It ends with a RETURN statement. Call is made by a GOSUB statement. Arguments are not allowed.

Example

Subroutine reference:

```
40    GOSUB  100
 .
 .
 .
100
 .
 .
 .
120   RETURN
```

FORTRAN

A subroutine is a sequence of instructions that performs some desired operation whose result is incorporated into a main program. FORTRAN provides for two classes of subroutines; function subroutines and subroutine subprograms. Function subroutines differ from subroutine subprograms in that they always return a single result to the calling program, whereas a subroutine subprogram may return more than one value to the calling program.

Example

Subroutine reference:

```
 .
 .
 .
CALL CONVERT(A,B,C,D,NUMBER)
 .
 .
 .
```

Subroutine declaration:

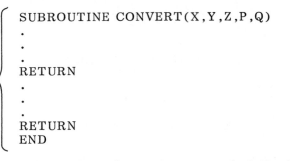

```
SUBROUTINE CONVERT(X,Y,Z,P,Q)
 .
 .
 .
RETURN
 .
 .
 .
RETURN
END
```

After the subroutine returns control to the calling program, the values under the variables X,Y,Z,P,Q will be assigned to the variables A,B,C,D,NUMBER, respectively.

PASCAL

A procedure is a self contained program segment starting with the word PROCEDURE. Procedures must be defined before their use (call) unless they are external or defined in a FORWARD statement. They can be structured as subroutines and are called by merely referring to their name. The type of the parameters must be defined in the procedure declaration. Note that the difference between a subroutine reference and a function reference is the fact that no result value is produced when a subroutine call is used.

Example

Procedure definition:
```
  PROCEDURE CONVERT(VAR M,Y,F,I:
                    INTEGER; INS:
                    INTEGER);
     .
     .
     .
  BEGIN
     .
     .
     .
  END;
```

Procedure reference:
```
     .
     .
     .
  CONVERT(A,B,C,D,NUMBER);
     .
     .
     .
```

COBOL

ANSI COBOL supports separately compiled subroutine subprograms. The arguments of the subroutine are specified in a special section of the DATA DIVISION, the LINKAGE SECTION. Subroutines are called in the main program by a CALL statement.

Example

```
CALL 'CALCINT' USING VAL1, TERM1,STAT1
    ('CALCINT' PROGRAM)
PROCEDURE DIVISION USING VALUE,TERMS,
                        STATUS.
```

(See Remaining Languages on Following Page)

14. SUBROUTINES

PL/1

A subroutine has more than one statement and is compiled as a separate subprogram. It begins with a SUBROUTINE statement and ends with an END statement. One or more RETURN statements which have the effect of terminating execution of the subprogram and returning to point of call in the main program may be included in the subroutine subprogram at logical termination points. Call to subroutine is accomplished through the use of CALL statements.

Example

```
PROGRAM READ(input,output)
.
.
.
CALL Skipblanks
.
.
.
.
.
Procedure skipblanks;
    begin
      REPEAT
          read(ch);
      UNTIL ch=blank
end;
```

APL

Using a function within another function is a basic programming technique that simplifies programming. When used within another function, an unlimited function can be classified as a sub-routine.

Subroutine execution is controlled by the ordinary call and return structure, with unrestricted recursive calls allowed. Return from a subroutine is done by a GOTO to a nonexistent statement number, usually statement number zero e.g. $\rightarrow 0$.

ALGOL-60

A subroutine can be constructed by a procedure which is a self-contained program segment beginning with a PROCEDURE statement and consisting of one or more statements and/or blocks. The subroutine is called by stating the procedure name with appropriate arguments.

Refer to section 13-Functions (User defined).

Example

Procedure reference:
.
.
.
.

CONVERT(A,B,C,D,NUMBER);
.
.
.

Procedure definition:
```
    PROCEDURE CONVERT(X,Y,Z,P,Q);
        VALUE X,Y,Z,P,Q;
        REAL   X,Y,Z,P,Q;
        BEGIN
            .
            .
            .
            .
        END;
```

15. INTRINSIC/LIBRARY FUNCTIONS

BASIC

Intrinsic or Library functions can be used in the same manner as user defined functions. Notice all functions have three-letter names followed by an argument enclosed in parentheses. Below is a list of commonly available functions in BASIC.

FUNCTION	EXPLANATION
ABS(X)	Calculates absolute value of x.
SIN(X)	Calculates trigonometric sine of x, where x is in radians.
COS(X)	Calculates trigonometric cosine of x, where x is in radians.
TAN(X)	Calculates trigonometric tangent of x, where x is in radians.
ATN(X)	Calculates trigonometric arctangent of x, where result is in radians.
INT(X)	Calculates integer part of x.
EXP(X)	Calculates the exponential function, e^x.
LOG(X)	Calculates natural logarithm (base e) of x.
LGT(X)	Calculates common logarithm (base 10) of x.
SQR(X)	Calculates square root of x, $\sqrt{x}$.
SGN(X)	Determines the sign of x.
RND(X)	Generates a random number between 0 and 1.

FORTRAN

Intrinsic or Library functions can be used in the same way as user defined functions. Fortran permits great flexibility in the use of its functions. Any valid expression may be used as an argument of a function. A set of commonly used functions is listed below.

FUNCTION		EXPLANATION
INTEGER	REAL	
IABS (J)	ABS(X)	Calculates absolute value of J/x; $|J|$, $|x|$.
	SIN(X)	Calculates trigonometric sine of x, where x is in radians.
	COS(X)	Calculates trigonometric cosine of x, where x is in radians.
	TAN(X)	Calculates trigonometric tangent of x, where x is in radians.
	ATAN(X)	Calculates trigonometric arctangent of x, where result is in radians.
	EXP(X)	Calculates the exponential function, e^x.
	ALOG(X)	Calculates natural logarithm (base e) of x.
	ALOG10(X)	Calculates common logarithm (base 10) of x.
	SQRT(X)	Calculates square root of x, $\sqrt{x}$. x is a real valued expression.

PASCAL

Intrinsic or Library functions can be used in the same way as user-defined functions. The standard functions are listed and explained below.

Arithmetic functions:

FUNCTION	EXPLANATION
ABS(X)	Calculates absolute value of x, $\lvert x \rvert$.
SIN(X)	Calculates trigonometric sine of x, where x is in radians.
COS(X)	Calculates trigonometric cosine of x, where x is in radians.
ARCTAN(X)	Calculates trigonometric arctangent of x, where the result is in radians.
EXP(X)	Calculates the exponential function of x, e^x.
LN(X)	Calculates natural logarithm (base e) of x.
SQRT(X)	Calculates square root of x, $\sqrt{x}$.
SQR(X)	Calculates square of x, x*x.

Boolean functions:

FUNCTION	EXPLANATION
ODD(X)	The type of x must be integer; the result is true if x is odd, otherwise false.
EOLN(X)	Returns the value true when, while reading text file F, the end of current line is reached, otherwise false.
EOF(X)	Returns the value true when, while reading the file F, the "end-of-file" is reached, otherwise false.

Transfer functions:

FUNCTION	EXPLANATION
TRUNC(X)	x must be of type real, the result is the greatest integer less

COBOL

Not Applicable.

(Continued on Page 65)

(See Remaining Languages on Following Page)

15. INTRINSIC/LIBRARY FUNCTIONS

PL/1

Intrinsic functions can be used in the same manner as user defined function-type procedures. In PL/1 they are called built-in functions, of which there are a large number (see appendix III). Many of these are generic; this means that the same name can be used for differing types of arguments. Almost every built-in function has a specified number of arguments. The functions can be divided into the following classifications. Arithmetic generic (e.g., ABS,MAX, and TRUNC); float arithmetic, which converts all input arguments to floating point before the function is invoked and produces floating point numbers as results(e.g. LOG2,SIND, which are defined only for real arguments, and SIN,LOG,and SQRT, which are defined for real and complex arguments); string generic(e.g., BIT, SUBSTR, and BOOL); array manipulation, which has array expressions with scalar values as arguments but no arrays of structures(e.g.,SUM, POLY, and LBOUND). All the built-in functions in the arithmetic and string generic categories may have array or structure expressions as arguments except where integer decimal constants are required, and they yield arrays or structures as results; condition (e.g., ONFILE, ONCHAR, ONKEY), list processing (ADDR and NULL), and the miscellaneous category (DATE, TIME, LINENO, EVENT, and PRIORITY).

(for examples see appendix VI)

APL

The elementary APL functions $(+,-,\times,\div)$ are generally referred to as scalar functions. However, much of the power of the APL language is demonstrated by the ability to extend these elementary functions, along with a comprehensive set of additional functions, to vectors and higher order arrays of data. The scalar monadic functions (i.e. one argument) can operate element by element on a single array. Likewise, the scalar dyadic (i.e. two argument) functions can operate pairwise on matching elements of two vectors or higher order arrays which have the same shape.

There is also an extensive set of mixed (i.e. non-scalar) functions in APL which operate non-pairwise on vectors or higher order arrays of possibly different shapes.

Example

The non-scalar function 'reshape" (symbol ρ) is used to create an array as follows:

```
    BS←3 2ρ7 1.5 ¯4 8.01 1 9
    BS
 7  1.5
¯4  8.01
 1  9
```

Statements of the above form (i.e. M Nρ Data) create an M by N matrix which consists of the data listed to the right of the reshape function. Reshape can also be used to create vectors as follows:

```
    cc←5ρ9
    cc
99999
```

(Refer to appendix VII for a list of APL functions).

PASCAL

	than or equal to x for x $\geq$ 0, and the least integer greater or equal to x for x $<$ 0.
ROUND(X)	x must be of type real; the result, of type integer, is the value x rounded.
ORD(X)	The ordinal number of the argument x in the set of values defined by type of x.
CHR(X)	x must be of type integer and the result is the character whose ordinal number is x (if it exists).

Further standard functions:

FUNCTION	EXPLANATION
SUCC(X)	x is of any type (except real), and the result is the successor value of x (if it exists).
PRED(X)	x is of any scalar type (except real), and the result is the predecessor value of x (if it exists).

ALGOL-60

Library functions can be accessed in the same manner as function-type procedures.

Examples

Absolute value:
      Y:=ABS(X);
Square root:
      ROOT:=SQRT(A+B);
Truncation:
      J:=ENTIER(X/Y)+1;

C

Intrinsic or Library functions can be accessed in the same manner as user-defined functions.

Example

(1) Square root:
      ROOT=SQRT(A*B)
(2) COS(X)   Calculates trigonometric cosine of X, where
                X is in radians.

16. INPUT/OUTPUT

BASIC

I/O is achieved by INPUT and PRINT statements. Data is entered in free form with commas as separators.

Examples

Input statement:
```
    10 INPUT A,J,I,V,N$
```
Corresponding input data:(to be typed in from the keyboard of the terminal)
```
    313791,5328,3145680,-506,JAMES
```

Output statement:
```
    20 PRINT A; "IS A PRIME NUMBER"
```
Corresponding output:
```
    313791 IS A PRIME NUMBER
```

(See READ and DATA statements in 11.)

FORTRAN

I/O is achieved by READ, WRITE, and FORMAT statements. Unformatted I/O is implementation dependent.

Examples

Formatted input statements:
```
    READ(5,9)I,J,A,VAL
9   FORMAT(I6,I5,10X,2I7)
```

Corresponding input data:
```
    313791 ƀ5328 ƀƀƀƀƀƀƀƀƀ3145680 ƀƀƀ-506
```

Formatted output statements:
```
    WRITE(6,10)I
10  FORMAT(1X,I6,'IS A PRIME NUMBER')
```

Corresponding output:
```
    ƀ313791 IS A PRIME NUMBER
```

PASCAL

Built-in I/O procedures of Pascal are READ, READLN, WRITE and WRITELN for files of char- acters (TEXTFILES) and GET and PUT for any typed file. There are two standard TEXTFILE titles INPUT and OUTPUT identified with stand- ard I/O media of the computer installation. They are considered as default values in text-file op- erations. Formatted output is standard but formatted input is implementation dependent.

Examples

Declaration statements:

```
VAR   R,S : REAL;
      I,J : INTEGER;
      C,D : CHAR;
```

Input statements:

```
READ(C,D);
READLN(J,S);
READ(I,R);
```

Corresponding input data:

```
ABb-16b-4.02E5
15b3.1
```

Output statements:

```
WRITELN(C);
WRITE(S,J,D);
```

Corresponding output:

```
A
-4.02E5  -16  B
```

COBOL

Data files are named and allocated to hardware devices on which they are to be read or written in the INPUT-OUTPUT SECTION of the ENVI- RONMENT DIVISION. Data-file descriptions and their record descriptions are contained in the DATA DIVISION. Record file oriented I/O is achieved with OPEN, CLOSE, READ, and WRITE statements in the PROCEDURE DIVISION. Data- oriented I/O is achieved with ACCEPT and DISPLAY statements in the PROCEDURE DIVISION.

Examples

Environment Division entries:

```
INPUT-OUTPUT SECTION.
FILE-CONTROL.
      SELECT INPUT-FILE ASSIGN TO
            CARD-READER.
      SELECT OUTPUT-FILE ASSIGN TO
            PRINTER.
```

Data Division entries:

```
FILE SECTION.
FD INPUT-FILE LABEL RECORDS OMITTED
            DATA RECORD IS INPUT-REC.
01    INPUT-REC.
      02    NAME-IN        PIC X(15).
      02    SEX-CODE       PIC 9.
      02    SALARY-IN      PIC 99999V99.
FD OUTPUT-FILE LABEL RECORDS OMITTED
            DATA RECORD IS OUTPUT-REC.
01    OUTPUT-REC.
      02    FILLER         PIC X(132).
```

Procedure Division entries:

```
MAIN-LOGIC.
      OPEN INPUT INPUT-FILE
            OUTPUT OUTPUT-FILE.
      READ INPUT-FILE AT END
            GO TO FINISH.
      WRITE OUTPUT-REC.
FINISH.
      CLOSE INPUT-FILE OUTPUT-FILE.
```

(See Remaining Languages on Following Page)

16. INPUT/OUTPUT

PL/1

PL/1 has a formidable battery of I/O facilities. Record file oriented I/O is achieved with READ and WRITE statements similar to those found in COBOL. For stream files where data-type conversions take place to meet the attributes of the variables, the basic I/O statements are GET and PUT. There are three forms of these statements: LIST-directed, DATA-directed and EDIT-directed. The first two forms are unformatted.

In LIST-directed form the programmer specifies a list of variable names whose values are to be transmitted. The input-output file contains only values in this case. For input, the values must be on the external file in sequence separated by blanks or commas, but on output the separator between items is the blank.

Examples

Input statement:

```
    GET LIST(I,J,A,VAL);
```
Corresponding input:
```
    313791, 5238, 3145680.0,-506.2
```

Output statement:
```
    PUT LIST(I,J,A,VAL);
```
Corresponding output:
```
    313791ƀ5238ƀ3145680.0ƀ-506.2
```

In DATA-directed form each data item consists of a series of assignment statements without semicolons, separated by commas or blanks. Each series is terminated with a semicolon. On output, only blanks are used to separate data items, and the last item is followed by a semicolon.

Examples

Input statement:
```
    GET DATA(CITY,TEMP-MAX,TEMP-MIN);
```
Corresponding input data:
```
    CITY='NEW YORK',TEMP-MAX=72.6,TEMP-
    MIN=-6.5;
```

APL

Most APL systems are equipped with various system functions which are used to produce formatted output. The 'quad'symbol ⎕ and the 'quote- quad' symbol ⍞ are used to create user-defined interactive functions. The function of ⎕ is to put the system in evaluated input mode. The system will display the prompt '⎕:' and wait for numeric or character data to be input from the keyboard while in evaluated input mode. Input data must be enclosed in single quotes when in evaluated input mode. Likewise, ⍞ puts the system in character input mode. Quotes are not used when entering data when the system is in character input mode. A prompt is not displayed when in character input mode.

The following interactive function demonstrates the use of 'quote-quad':

```
    ∇NONSENSE
[1] 'WHAT IS YOUR NAME?'
[2] NAME←⍞
[3] ' ' ◊ 'HELLO', NAME,'!'
[4] 'THERE ARE ',(⍕⍴NAME),'LETTERS IN YOUR NAME.'
[5] (⍕+/NAMEε'AEIOU'),' OF THESE LETTERS ARE VOWELS.'
[6] (⍕+/NAMEε'NICE'), ' LETTERS IN YOUR NAME ARE'
[7] 'COMMON TO THE WORD "NICE".'
[8]∇
```

```
SAMPLE OUTPUT:

    NONSENSE
WHAT IS YOUR NAME?
BRUCE

HELLO BRUCE!
THERE ARE 5 LETTERS IN YOUR NAME.
2 OF THESE LETTERS ARE VOWELS.
2 LETTERS IN YOUR NAME ARE
COMMON TO THE WORD 'NICE'.
```

Most implementations of APL are supplied with powerful component filing systems. A file in APL is accessed by a number (i.e. tie). All file operations are performed with an extensive set of system functions. APL files are independent of the workspace being used.

 (Continued on Page 70)

ALGOL-60

ALGOL-60 does not include standardized I/O procedures. Considerable variation exists from one version of the language to another. Some versions use unformatted input procedures and formatted output procedures. Other versions make use of specialized I/O procedures such as shown below.

Example

```
READ(X,Y[3],NAME);
    Corresponding input data:
-3, 2.39, "GABRIEL"

BEGIN
    SPACE (6) ; PRINT (X,5);
    SPACE (6) ; PRINT (Y[3],0.3);
    SPACE (12) ; WRITE (NAME);

BEGIN PAGE;
    SPACE ; WRITE ("x= ");
    PRINT (X,2.6)
    SPACE (6); WRITE ("y=   ");
    PRINT (M,2.6);
    SPACE (6); WRITE ("y=   ");
    PRINT (Y,2.6);
    NEWLINE END;
```

C

C provides no input-output facilities: There are no READ or WRITE statements and no wired-in file access methods. All of these higher-level mechanisms must be provided by explicitly-called functions.

Standard Input and Output-Getchar and Putchar: The simplest input mechanism is to read a character at a time from the "standard input", generally the user's terminal, with getchar. Getchar() returns the next input character each time it is called. In most environments that support C, a file may be substituted for the terminal using the < convention: if a program prog uses getchar, then the command line prog <infile causes prog to read infile instead of the terminal. Getchar returns the value EOF when it encounters end of file on whatever input is being read.

For output, putchar(c) puts the character c on the "standard output", which is also by default the terminal. The output can be directed to a file by using >: if prog uses putchar, Prog>outfile will write the standard output onto outfile instead of the terminal.

Output produced by printf also finds its way to the standard output and calls to putchar and printf may be interleaved.

Formatted Output - Printf: The two routines printf for output and scanf for input permit translation to and from character representations of numerical quantities. They also allow generation or interpretation of formatted lines.

$$printf(control, arg1, arg2, ...).$$

Here printf converts, formats and prints its arguments on the standard output under control of the string control. The control string contains two types of objects: ordinary characters, which are simply copied to the output stream and conversion specifications, each of which causes conversion and printing of the next successive argument to printf.

Each conversion specification is introduced by the character % and ended by a conversion character.

Between the % and the conversion character there may be:

(Continued on page 70)   69

16. INPUT/OUTPUT

PL/1

Output statement:

> PUT DATA(CITY,TEMP-MIN,TEMP-MAX);

Corresponding output:

> CITY='NEW YORK'   TEMP-MIN=-6.5
> TEMP-MAX=72.6;

The EDIT-directed form utilizes a programmer-supplied format which specifies the exact data type conversions needed for each data item. Format terms can be included in the GET and PUT statements or can appear in separate FORMAT statements.

Examples

Input statement:
    GET EDIT(A,WORD,I,J)(F(5,2),A(10),2F(7));
Corresponding input data:
    42.32CALIFORNIA37304255240373

Output statement:
    PUT EDIT(A,WORD,J,I)(F(5),A(10),2F(7));
Corresponding output:
    42CALIFORNIA52403733730425

Output statement:
    PUT EDIT('C:',C)(R(FORM));
    FORM:FORMAT(SKIP,COLUMN(3),A(2),X(3),
              5F(7,4));
Corresponding output:
  ƀƀc:ƀƀƀ21.8500ƀƀƀ142.7000ƀƀƀ62.500ƀƀƀ181.4000ƀƀƀ99.2500

C

A minus sign, specifies left adjustment of the converted argument in its field.

A digit string specifying a minimum field width.

A period, which separates the field from the next digit string.

A digit string (the precision), which specifies the maximum number of characters to be printed from a string or the number of digits to be printed to the right of the decimal point of a float or double.

The conversion characters and their meanings are:

d   The argument is converted to decimal notation.

o   The argument is converted to unsigned octal notation (without a leading zero).

x   The argument is converted to unsigned hexadecimal notation (without a leading ox).

u   The argument is converted to unsigned decimal notation.

c   The argument is taken to be a single character.

s   The argument is a string; characters from the sting are printed until a null character is reached or until the number of characters indicated by the precision specification is exhausted.

e   The argument is taken to be a float or double and converted to decimal notation of the form [-]m.nnnnnn E[±]xx where the length of the string of n's is specified by the precision. The default precision is 6.

f   The argument is taken to be a float or

double and converted to decimal notation of the form [-]mmm.nnnnn where the length of the string of n's is specified by the precision. The default precision is 6. Note that the precision does not determine the number of significant digits printed in f format.

g   Use % e or % f, whichever is shorter; non-significant zeros are not printed.

Example

```
: % 10s:        :hello, world:
: % -10s:       :hello, world:
: % 20s:        :       hello, world:
: % -20s:       :hello, world        :
: % 20.10s:     :       hello, wor:
: % -20.10s:    :hello, wor          :
: % .10s:       :hello, wor:
```

Formatted Input-Scanf: The function scanf is the input analog of printf, providing many of the same conversation facilities in the opposite direction.

scanf(control,arg1,arg2,...).

Scanf reads characters from the standard input, interprets them according to the format specified in control, and stores the results in the remaining arguments.

The control string usually contains conversion specifications, which are used to direct interpretation of input sequences. The control string may contain:

Blanks, tabs or newlines ("white space characters") which are ignored.

Ordinary characters (not %) which are expected to match the next non-white space character of the input stream.

Conversion specifications, consisting of the character % an optional assignment suppression character *, an optional number specifying a

maximum field width, and a conversion character.

The other arguments, each of which must be a pointer, indicate where the corresponding converted input should be stored.

The conversion character indicates the interpretation of the input field, the corresponding argument must be a pointer as required by the call by value semantics of C.

The following conversion characters are legal:

d   A decimal is expected in the input; the corresponding argument should be an integer pointer.

o   an octal integer (with or without a leading zero) is expected in the input, the corresonding argument should be an integer pointer.

x   a hexadecimal integer (with or without a leading ox) is expected in the input; the corresponding argument should be an integer pointer.

h   a short integer is expected in the input; the corresponding argument should be a pointer to a short integer.

c   a single character is expected; the corresponding argument should be a character pointer; the next input character is placed at the indicated spot. The normal skip over white space characters are suppressed in this case; to read the next non-white space character, use % 1s.

s   a character string is expected, the corresponding argument should be a character pointer pointing to an array of characters large enough to accept the string and a terminating \0 will be added.

f   a floating point number is expected; the corresponding argument should be a

(Continued on page 72)   71

C

pointer to a float. The conversion character e is a synonym for f. The input format for float is an optional sign, a string of numbers possibly containing a decimal point and an optional exponent field containing an E or e followed by a possibly signed integer.

Example

```
int i ;
float x ;
char name [50] ;
scanf ("%d%f%s", &i,name);
```
with input line
```
25    54.32E-1  VIJAY
```
will assign the value 25 to i, the value of 5.43 to x and the string "VIJAY" properly terminated by \0, to name.

In-memory Format conversion: The functions scanf and printf have siblings called sscanf and sprintf which perform the corresponding conversions, but operate on a string instead of a file.
The general format is
```
sprintf(string,control,arg1,arg2,...)
sscanf(string,control,arg1,arg2,...)
```

Example

```
sprintf (name, "temp %d",n);
```
creates a string of the form temp nnn in name, where nnn is the value of n.
sscanf does the reverse conversions. The call
```
sscanf(name, "temp %d",&n);
```
sets n to the value of the string of digits following temp in name.

PASCAL

Not applicable.

COBOL

STOP, statement causes temporary suspension of program execution. The STOP RUN statement causes immediate termination of the program.

ALGOL-60

Not applicable. Blocks are executed sequentially in ALGOL-60.

C

Not applicable.

18. DOCUMENTATION

BASIC

Documentation can be provided by a REM statement.

Example

10   REM THIS IS A BASIC REMARK

A remark can appear on the same line as a statement provided it starts with an apostrophe.

Example

50   GOSUB 300 'LOOKUP

FORTRAN

A card (line) in a FORTRAN program will be treated as a comment card(line) if column 1 contains a C. Its contents will be ignored by the compiler.

Example

C   THIS IS A FORTRAN COMMENT

PL/1

Comments can be inserted anywhere in the program provided they are enclosed by the symbols /* and */.

Example

/* THIS IS A PL/1 COMMENT */

APL

Comment statements are made by placing ⍝ before the statement. (This composite symbol is formed by keying in ∩, backspacing, then keying in 0). Comment statements are useful for putting your name on assignments, numbering exercises and inserting comments within your programs.

Example

⍝   JOE DOE
⍝   1.
     (3*2) + (6x7)
51.

PASCAL

Comments can be inserted anywhere in the program provided they are enclosed by the symbols { } or (* *) depending on the implementation.

Example

(* THIS IS A PASCAL COMMENT *) or
{THIS IS A PASCAL COMMENT}

COBOL

Comments can be added to the PROCEDURE DIVISION by using a NOTE statement.

Example

NOTE   THIS IS A COBOL NOTE.

ALGOL-60

Comments can be inserted anywhere in the program by means of the comment statement.

Example

COMMENT CONVERSION ROUTINE;

C

Comments can be inserted anywhere in the program provided they are enclosed by the symbols /* and */. Comments do not nest. Comments can appear anywhere that a blank or newline can appear.

Example

/* THIS IS A C COMMENT */

SAMPLE PROGRAM I

PROBLEM

From numerical values of a salesman's weekly pay and his sales for the past week, compute his total weekly pay, which is his weekly base pay plus 4 percent of all weekly sales over $100.00.

BASIC

```
10      INPUT B,S
20      IF S>100 THEN 50
30      LET C=0
40      GOTO 60
50      LET C=0.04 * (S-100)
60      LET P=B+C
70      PRINT " TOTAL PAY IS "; P
80      END
```

```
          ?
Input Data:
     82.50, 476.13
```

Output Data:
     TOTAL PAY IS 97.545

When the above program is executed, a question mark "?" appears on the monitor screen. This is caused by the INPUT statement of line number 10. The "?" indicates that the program expects a response from the user. The user must know that he has to type in the values for the salesman's basic pay and his sales.

In some versions of BASIC, a string can be included in the INPUT statement before the variables which will then tell the user what he or she has to type in. In the above example, the statement 10 can be replaced by
     10 INPUT "ENTER Weekly base pay, weekly sales"; B,S

FORTRAN

```
        READ(5,10)B,S
10      FORMAT(F6.2,F7.2)
        IF(S.GT.100.) GOTO 20
        C=0
        GO TO 30
20      C=0.04 * (S-100.)
30      P=B+C
        WRITE(6,40)P
40      FORMAT(1X,'TOTAL PAY IS',F6.3)
        STOP
        END
```

Input Data:
     ϸ82.50, ϸ476.13

Output:
     TOTAL PAY IS 97.545

The general form of the READ statement in standard FORTRAN is

$$READ(i,n)$$

where i is an integer which represents an input device and n is the statement number of the FORMAT statement. In this program, we have used the input device number 5 for the keyboard. Hence when this program is executed the user has to type the values for B and S from the keyboard.

In some versions of FORTRAN IV, a special case of the READ statement can be used in which the input device-keyboard is implied. Such a READ statement is the ACCEPT statement. In ACCEPT statement, the input device number need not be specified since it is implied.

In the above program, the first statement can be replaced by the following statement.
     ACCEPT(10), B,S

The brackets are optional.

PASCAL

```
PROGRAM PAY (INPUT, OUPUT);
VAR B,S,P:REAL;
BEGIN
    READ(B,S);
    IF(S>100.0)THEN
    C:=0.04 * (S-100.0)
    ELSE
    C:=0;
    P:=B+C;
    WRITELN ('TOTAL PAY IS', P)
END.
```

Input Data:
       82.50 ⌀ 476.13

Output:
       TOTAL PAY IS 0.9754518E02

The first statement of this program indicates that the program expects some input data, and also it will print output data. The VAR statement declares that the two input variables B and S and the output variable P are real. The READ statement READ(B,S), reads two values from an input medium and assigns these values to the variables B and S. The input medium can be a data file or it can be entered from the keyboard of a terminal. The main block of the program is a compound statement starting with BEGIN and terminating with the END.

COBOL

```
IDENTIFICATION DIVISION .
PROGRAM-ID. PAY.
ENVIRONMENT DIVISION.
CONFIGURATION SECTION.
SOURCE-COMPUTER . DECSYSTEM-10.
OBJECT-COMPUTER . DECSYSTEM-10.
INPUT-OUTPUT SECTION.
FILE CONTROL.
    SELECT CARD-FILE ASSIGN TO CARD-READER.
    SELECT PRINT-FILE ASSIGN TO PRINTER.
DATA DIVISION.
FD CARD-FILE,
    LABEL RECORDS ARE OMITTED
    DATA RECORD IS CARD-IN.
01  CARD-IN.
    02 BASIC PIC 999V99.
    02 SALES PIC 999V99.
FD PRINT-FILE
    LABEL RECORDS ARE OMITTED
    DATA RECORD IS PRINT-LINE.
01  PRINT-LINE.
    02 FILLER  PIC X(132).


WORKING-STORAGE SECTION.
01   COMMISSION   PIC 9(4)V99 VALUE ZERO.
01   TOTAL        PIC 9(4)V99 VALUE ZERO.
01   END-OF-DATA PIC XXX      VALUE 'NO'.

01   HEADER.
       02 FILLER PIC X(15) VALUE SPACES.
       02 FILLER PIC X(12) VALUE IS
          'TOTAL PAY IS'.
01   DATA-LINE.
       02 FILLER PIC X(15) VALUE SPACES.
       02 TOTAL-PAY PIC $$$9.99.


PROCEDURE DIVISION.
MAIN-LOGIC.
       OPEN INPUT CARD-FILE,
           OUTPUT PRINT-FILE
       WRITE PRINT-LINE FROM HEADER
           AFTER ADVANCING 5 LINES
       PERFORM READ-CARD
       PERFORM PROCESS UNTIL
           END-OF-DATA = 'YES'
       CLOSE CARD-FILE,
           PRINT-FILE
       STOP RUN.

READ-CARD.
       READ CARD-FILE RECORD
           AT END
               MOVE 'YES' TO END-OF-DATA.
```

(Continued on Page 81)   79

SAMPLE PROGRAM I

PL/1

```
PAY:          PROCEDURE OPTIONS(MAIN);
              GET DATA(B,S);
              IF S>100 THEN GOTO COMMISSION;
              C=0;
              GOTO TOT-PAY;
COMMISSION:   C=0.04 * (S-100);
TOT-PAY:      P=B+C;
              PUT DATA(P);
              END PAY;
```

In this example, we have used the Data Directed transmission of input data. In this case, the input data has to be in the form of assignment statements, separated by commas or blanks. Input/output formatting can also be done. This is accomplished by the GET EDIT and PUT EDIT statements. Format terms can be included in the GET and PUT statements or can appear in separate Format statements.

APL

```
     ∇   PAY
[1]  'ENTER BASE PAY'
[2]  B←▯
[3]  'ENTER SALES'
[4]  S←▯
[5]  →8×ι (S>100)
[6]  C←0
[7]  →9
[8]  C←0.04×(S-100)
[9]  P←B+C
[10] 'TOTAL PAY IS'
[11] P
[12]∇
```

The statement [2] is an Input statement which expects a value from an Input medium (usually the keyboard of a terminal). When this value is entered, it is assigned to the variable B. Statement [5] is a conditional branch statement which branches to the line number 8 if the value of S is greater than 100. The multiplication and the symbol ι (lower case iota) can be treated as IF.

COBOL

```
PROCESS.
     MOVE ZERO TO COMMISSION.
     IF SALES > 100.0
          COMPUTE COMMISSION=0.04*(SALES-100.0).
     ADD BASIC,COMMISSION GIVING TOTAL.
     MOVE TOTAL TO TOTAL-PAY.
     WRITE PRINT-LINE FROM DATA-LINE,
          BEFORE ADVANCING 1 LINE.
     PERFORM READ-CARD.
```

Input Data:
       0825047613

Output: .

        .

        .

        .

        .

        TOTAL PAY IS
        b$97.54

ALGOL-60

```
begin
     real B,S,C,P;
     READ(B,S);
     if S >100 then goto AB
     else
          begin
               C:=0;
               goto CD;
          end
AB:  C:= 0.04x(S-100);
CD:  P:= B+C;
     PRINT(P);
end
```

Note that ALGOL-60 does not include standardized I/O procedures. Considerable variation exists from one version of the language to another. Some versions of ALGOL-60 utilize formatted I/O procedures similar to those used in Fortran.

C

```
main ()
{
     float b,s,p,c;
     scanf(" %f %f",&b,&s);
     if(s >100){
       c=0.04 * (s-100);
       p=b+c;
     }else{
          c=0;
          p=b+c;
     }
     printf("Total pay is %f", P);
}
```

The float statement declares the variables b,s and p as floating point variables. Scanf reads characters from the standard input (usually the keyboard of a terminal) and interprets them according to the format specified in the control field (enclosed in the double quotation marks) and stores the results in the remaining arguments. Printf is the analog of scanf. It converts, formats and prints its arguments on the standard output. The character "{ " is similar to BEGIN in the Pascal compound statement and "}" is similar to the END statement of Pascal.

SAMPLE PROGRAM II

PROBLEM

An 8 GHz (frequency of the transmitting wave of the RADAR) Police Radar measures a Doppler frequency of F Hz from a car approaching the stationary police vehicle in an S miles/hour speed limit zone. The Doppler frequency in hertz and the speed limit in miles/hour are fed as the input to the computer. Write a program which takes the Doppler frequency and the speed limit as the input, and displays the warning message "CHASE THE CAR" to the policeman, as its output when the car is moving at a speed greater than S miles/hour.

SOLUTION WORKED OUT IN LONGHAND
(Without Computers)

The speed of the car can be calculated by using the formula $F = 2S/\lambda$, where F is the Doppler frequency, λ is the wavelength of the transmitting wave, and S is the speed of the car. If F is in Hz and λ is in meters, then S will be in meters/sec. λ is given by $\lambda = v/f$, where v is the velocity of light (3×10^8 m/sec) and f is the frequency of the transmitting wave = 8 GHz ($= 8 \times 10^9$ Hz) in this case.

$$\lambda = \frac{v}{f} = \frac{3 \times 10^8}{8 \times 10^9} = 0.0375 \text{m}.$$

$$\lambda/2 = 0.01875 \text{m}.$$

$$S = \text{Speed of Car} = \frac{\lambda F}{2}$$

$$= (F * 0.01875) \text{ m/sec}.$$
$$= (0.04194256 * F) \text{ miles/hour}.$$

BASIC

```
10    REM PROGRAM FOR ENFORCING SPEED LIMIT
20    PRINT "TYPE THE DOPPLER FREQUENCY IN Hz";
30    PRINT "AND SPEED LIMIT IN MILES PER HOUR";
40    PRINT "SEPARATED BY A COMMA"
50    INPUT F,V
60    REM SPEED OF CAR IN MILES/HOUR
70    Let S = 0.0419 * F
80    REM COMPARE WITH V
90    IF S< = V THEN GOTO 120
100   REM WARNING MESSAGE
110   PRINT "CHASE THE CAR"
120   END
```

FORTRAN

```
C     PROGRAM FOR ENFORCING SPEED LIMIT
      WRITE (6,10)
10    FORMAT(1X, 'TYPE DOPPLER FREQ.,SPEED'
     -' LIMIT')
      READ (5,20) F,V
20    FORMAT (2F10.2)
C     CALCULATE SPEED OF CAR
      S = 0.0419 * F
      IF(S.LE.V) GOTO 40
      WRITE(6,30)
30    FORMAT(3X,'CHASE THE CAR')
40    STOP
      END
```

PL/1

```
PROCEDURE;
/* Read the values of Doppler frequency
                and speed limit*/
    GET (F,V);
    S = 0.0419 * F
    IF S < = V THEN GOTO SAFE;
    PUT LIST ('CHASE THE CAR');
SAFE: END;
```

APL

```
    ∇RADAR
[1] 'ENTER DOPPLER FREQUENCY'
[2] F←⎕
[3] 'ENTER SPEED LIMIT'
[4] V←⎕
[5] S←0.0419×F
[6] →9×ι (S<V)
[7] 'CHASE THE CAR'
[8]∇
```

PASCAL

```
PROGRAM RADAR(INPUT,OUTPUT);
LABEL 50;
VAR S,F,V : REAL;
BEGIN
    READ(F,V);
    S : = 0.0419 * F;
    IF S <=V THEN GOTO 50
    ELSE
    WRITELN('CHASE THE CAR')
50: END.
```

COBOL

```
IDENTIFICATION DIVISION.
PROGRAM-ID. CHASE.
REMARKS. THIS PROGRAM ENFORCES SPEED LIMIT
        F   IS THE DOPPLER FREQUENCY
        V   IS THE SPEED LIMIT
        S   IS THE SPEED OF THE CAR.

BEGIN-PARA.
    ACCEPT F,V FROM CONSOLE.

COMPUTING-PARA.
    COMPUTE S = 0.0419 * F
    IF S > V
        DISPLAY "CHASE THE CAR" UPON CONSOLE
    ELSE
        GO TO END-PARA.

END-PARA.

    STOP RUN.
```

ALGOL-60

```
begin
    real F,V,S;
    READ(F,V);
    COMMENT   speed in miles/hour;
    S = 0.0419 * F;
    if S < = V then goto OVER;
    WRITE ( "CHASE THE CAR");
OVER:   COMMENT End of Routine
    end
```

C

```
main ()

{

    float f, v,s;
    printf ("Type frequency, speed limit");
    scanf ("% f %f ", &f, &v);
    s = 0.0419 *f
    if ( s>v) printf ("chase the car");

}
```

PASCAL DELIMITER WORDS

AND
ARRAY
BEGIN
CASE
CONST
DIV
DO
DOWNTO
ELSE
END
FILE
FOR
FUNCTION
GOTO
IF
IN
LABEL
MOD
NIL
NOT
OF
OR
PACKED
PROCEDURE
PROGRAM
RECORD
REPEAT
SET
THEN
TO
TYPE
UNTIL
VAR
WHILE
WITH

APPENDIX II

ANSI COBOL RESERVED WORDS

ACCEPT	DATA	FOOTING
ACCESS	DATE	FOR
ADD	DATE-COMPILED	FROM
ADVANCING	DATE-WRITTEN	GENERATE
AFTER	DAY	GIVING
ALL	DE	GO
ALPHABETIC	DEBUG-CONTENTS	GREATER
ALSO	DEBUG-ITEM	GROUP
ALTER	DEBUG-LINE	HEADING
ALTERNATE	DEBUG-NAME	HIGH-VALUE
AND	DEBUG-SUB-1	HIGH-VALUES
ARE	DEBUG-SUB-2	I-O
AREA	DEBUG-SUB-3	I-O-CONTROL
AREAS	DEBUGGING	IDENTIFICATION
ASCENDING	DECIMAL-POINT	IF
ASSIGN	DECLARATIVES	IN
AT	DELETE	INDEX
AUTHOR	DELIMITED	INDEXED
BEFORE	DELIMITER	INDICATE
BLANK	DEPENDING	INITIAL
BLOCK	DESCENDING	INITIATE
BOTTOM	DESTINATION	INPUT
BY	DETAIL	INPUT-OUTPUT
CALL	DISABLE	INSPECT
CANCEL	DISPLAY	INSTALLATION
CD	DIVIDE	INTO
CF	DIVISION	INVALID
CH	DOWN	IS
CHARACTER	DUPLICATES	JUST
CHARACTERS	DYNAMIC	JUSTIFIED
CLOCK-UNITS	EGI	KEY
CLOSE	ELSE	LABEL
COBOL	EMI	LAST
CODE	ENABLE	LEADING
CODE-SET	END	LEFT
COLLATING	END-OF-PAGE	LENGTH
COLUMN	ENTER	LESS
COMMA	ENVIRONMENT	LIMIT
COMMUNICATION	EOP	LIMITS
COMP	EQUAL	LINAGE
COMPUTATIONAL	ERROR ESI	LINAGE-COUNTER
COMPUTE	EVERY	LINE
CONFIGURATION	EXCEPTION	LINE-COUNTER
CONTAINS	EXIT	LINES
CONTROL	EXTEND	LINKAGE
CONTROLS	FD	LOCK
COPY	FILE	LOW-VALUE
CORR	FILE-CONTROL	LOW-VALUES
CORRESPONDING	FILLER	MEMORY
COUNT	FINAL	MERGE
CURRENCY	FIRST	MESSAGE

ANSI COBOL RESERVED WORDS

MODE	REEL	SUB-QUEUE-1
MODULES	REFERENCES	SUB-QUEUE-2
MOVE	RELATIVE	SUB-QUEUE-3
MULTIPLE	RELEASE	SUBTRACT
MULTIPLY	REMAINDER	SUM
NATIVE	REMOVAL	SUPPRESS
NEGATIVE	RENAMES	SYMBOLIC
NEXT	REPLACING	SYNC
NO	REPORT	SYNCHRONIZED
NOT	REPORTING	TABLE
NUMBER	REPORTS	TALLYING
NUMERIC	RERUN	TAPE
OBJECT-COMPUTER	RESERVE	TERMINAL
OCCURS	RESET	TERMINATE
OF	RETURN	TEXT
OFF	REVERSED	THAN
OMITTED	REWIND	THROUGH
ON	REWRITE	THRU
OPEN	RF	TIME
OPTIONAL	RH	TIMES
OR	RIGHT	TO
ORGANIZATION	ROUNDED	TOP
OUTPUT	RUN	TRAILING
OVERFLOW	SAME	TYPE
PAGE	SEARCH	UNIT
PAGE-COUNTER	SECTION	UNSTRING
PERFORM	SECURITY	UNTIL
PF	SEGMENT	UP
PH	SEGMENT-LIMIT	UPON
PIC	SELECT	USAGE
PICTURE	SEND	USE
PLUS	SENTENCE	USING
POINTER	SEPARATE	VALUE
POSITION	SEQUENCE	VALUES
POSITIVE	SEQUENTIAL	VARYING
PRINTING	SET	WHEN
PROCEDURE	SIGN	WITH
PROCEDURES	SIZE	WORDS
PROCEED	SORT	WORKING-STORAGE
PROGRAM	SORT-MERGE	WRITE
PROGRAM-ID	SOURCE	ZERO
QUEUE	SOURCE-COMPUTER	ZEROES
QUOTE	SPACE	ZEROS
QUOTES	SPACES	+
RANDOM	SPECIAL-NAMES	-
RD	STANDARD	.
READ	STANDARD-1	/
RECEIVE	START	..
RECORD	STATUS	
RECORDS	STOP	>
REDEFINES	STRING	<
		=

APPENDIX III

SUMMARY OF COBOL FORMATS

This appendix gives a summary for all Cobol Procedure Division statement formats included in this book. Complete formats for the Identification Division and for the [File-Control] paragraph of the Environment Division are also included. Following is a list of conventions used for these formats.

    1) Words enclosed in brackets [] are reserved words. If such a word is in all capitals it must be included in that format.

    2) Underlined words are to be supplied by the user.

    3) Words enclosed in braces { } are optional; if used they must be employed as shown.

    4) Items enclosed in parentheses ( ) indicate that only one of the items is to be chosen for that format.

    5) All indicated punctuation must be included.

    6) Comments enclosed by asterisks *...* are not part of the format.

Identification Division Formats:

    IDENTIFICATION DIVISION

     PROGRAM-ID . Program-Name .

     {[AUTHOR]. Comment-Item.}

     {[INSTALLATION]. Comment-Item.}

     {[DATE-WRITTEN]. Comment-Item.}

     {[DATE-COMPILED]. Comment-Item.}

     {[SECURITY]. Comment-Item.}

     {[REMARKS]. Comment-Item.}

Environment Division Formats, [File-Control] paragraph:

    SELECT   File-Name   * all files *

    ASSIGN TO   System-Name   * all files *

$$[\text{ACCESS IS}] \left(\begin{array}{c} [\text{SEQUENTIAL}] \\ [\text{RANDOM}] \end{array} \right) \quad \text{* required for random access *}$$

$$[\text{MULTIPLY}] \left(\begin{array}{c} \underline{\text{Data-Name \#1}} \\ \underline{\text{Literal \#1}} \end{array} \right) \quad [\text{BY}] \quad \underline{\text{Data-Name \#2}} \quad \{[\text{ROUNDED}]\}$$

SUMMARY OF COBOL FORMATS

[MULTIPLY] $\left(\dfrac{\text{Data-Name \#1}}{\text{Literal \#1}}\right)$ [BY]

$\left(\dfrac{\text{Data-Name \#2}}{\text{Literal \#2}}\right)$ [GIVING] Data-Name #3

{[ROUNDED]} {[On SIZE ERROR] Statement.}

[OPEN] $\left(\begin{array}{l}\text{[INPUT]}\\ \text{[OUTPUT]}\\ \text{[I-O]}\end{array}\right)$ File-Name.

[PERFORM] Paragraph-Name #1 {[THRU] Paragraph-Name #2 }.

[PERFORM] Paragraph-Name #2 {[THRU] Paragraph-Name #2 }

$\left(\dfrac{\text{Data-Name}}{\text{Integer}}\right)$ [TIMES].

[PERFORM] Paragraph-Name #1 {[THRU] Paragraph-Name #2 }

[UNTIL] Condition.

[PERFORM] Paragraph-Name #1 {[THRU] Paragraph-Name #2 }

[VARYING] Data-Name #1 [FROM] Data-Name #2

[BY] Data-Name #3 [UNTIL] condition.

[READ] File-Name {[INTO] Data-Name} $\left(\begin{array}{l}\text{[AT END]}\\ \text{[INVALID KEY]}\end{array}\right)$

Statement.

[STOP RUN].

[SUBTRACT] $\left(\dfrac{\text{Data-Name \#1}}{\text{Literal \#1}}\right)$ [FROM] Data-Name #2

{[ROUNDED]} {[On SIZE ERROR] Statement}.

[SUBTRACT] $\left(\dfrac{\text{Data-Name \#1}}{\text{Literal \#1}}\right)$ [FROM] $\left(\dfrac{\text{Data-Name \#2}}{\text{Literal \#2}}\right)$

[GIVING] Data-Name #3 {[ROUNDED]}

{[On SIZE ERROR] Statement}.

[WRITE] Record-Name {[FROM] Data-Name}

$$\left\{ \begin{pmatrix} [BEFORE] \\ [AFTER] \end{pmatrix} [ADVANCING] \begin{pmatrix} \text{Data-Name [LINES]} \\ \underline{\text{Integer}} \text{ [LINES]} \\ \underline{\text{Special}}\text{-Name} \end{pmatrix} \right\}$$

[WRITE] Record-Name {[FROM] Data-Name} [INVALID Key]

Statement.

[ACTUAL Key IS] Data-Name   *direct files only *

[NOMINAL Key IS] Data-Name   *IBM-indexed files only *

[RECORD Key IS] Data-Name   *indexed files only*

[SYMBOLIC Key IS] Data-Name   *indexed files only*

Procedure Division Statement Formats:

[ACCEPT] Data-Name $\left\{ [FROM] \begin{pmatrix} [CONSOLE] \\ \text{Mnemonic-Name} \end{pmatrix} \right\}$.

[ADD] $\begin{pmatrix} \text{Data-Name \#1} \\ \underline{\text{Literal \#1}} \end{pmatrix}$ [TO] Data-Name #2 {[ROUNDED]}

{[ON SIZE ERROR] Statement}.

[ADD] $\begin{pmatrix} \text{Data-Name \#1} \\ \underline{\text{Literal \#1}} \end{pmatrix} \begin{pmatrix} \text{Data-Name \#2} \\ \underline{\text{Literal \#2}} \end{pmatrix}$ [GIVING]

Data-Name #3 {[ROUNDED]} {[On SIZE ERROR] Statement}.

[CLOSE] File-Name #1 File Name #x.

[COMPUTE] Data-Name #1 {[ROUNDED]} = $\begin{pmatrix} \text{Data-Name \#2} \\ \underline{\text{Literal}} \\ \underline{\text{Arithmetic}}\text{-Expression} \end{pmatrix}$

[On SIZE ERROR Statement]

[DISPLAY] $\begin{pmatrix} \text{Data-Name \#1} \\ \underline{\text{Literal \#1}} \end{pmatrix} \begin{pmatrix} \text{Data-Name \#x} \\ \underline{\text{Literal \#x}} \end{pmatrix}$

$\left\{ [UPON] \begin{pmatrix} \text{Mnemonic-Name} \\ \underline{\text{[CONSOLE]}} \end{pmatrix} \right\}$

[DIVIDE] $\begin{pmatrix} \text{Data-Name \#1} \\ \underline{\text{Literal \#1}} \end{pmatrix}$ [INTO] Data-Name #2

{[ROUNDED]} {[On SIZE ERROR] Statement}.

SUMMARY OF COBOL FORMATS

[DIVIDE] $\left(\frac{\text{Data-Name \#1}}{\text{Literal \#1}}\right)$ $\left(\frac{[\text{INTO}]}{[\text{BY}]}\right)$ $\left(\frac{\text{Data-Name \#2}}{\text{Literal \#2}}\right)$

     [GIVING] Data-Name #3 {[ROUNDED]}

     {[On SIZE ERROR] Statement}.

[EXIT]

[GO TO] Paragraph-Name.

[GO TO] Paragraph-Name #1 Paragraph-Name #2

     Paragraph-Name #x [DEPENDING On] Data-Name.

[IF] Condition Statement.

[MOVE] $\left(\frac{\text{Data-Name \#1}}{\text{Literal}}\right)$ [TO] Data-Name #2

[MOVE] $\left(\begin{array}{c}[\text{CORR}]\\ [\text{CORRESPONDING}]\end{array}\right)$ Data-Name #1 [TO] Data-Name #2.

APPENDIX IV

PL/1 BUILT-IN FUNCTIONS

Arithmetic generic

    ABS
    MAX
    MIN
    MOD
    SIGN
    FIXED
    FLOAT
    FLOOR
    CEIL
    TRUNC
    BINARY
    DECIMAL
    PRECISION
    ADD
    MULTIPLY
    DIVIDE
    COMPLEX
    REAL
    IMAG
    CONJG

Float arithmetic generic

    EXP
    LOG
    LOG10
    LOG2
    ATAND
    ATAN
    TAND
    TAN
    SIND
    SIN
    COSD
    COS
    TANH
    ERF
    SQRT
    ERFC
    COSH
    SINH
    ATANH
    ATAN
    ATAND

String generic

    BIT
    CHAR
    SUBSTR

    INDEX
    LENGTH
    HIGH
    LOW
    REPEAT
    UNSPEC
    BOOL

Generic functions for manipulation of arrays

    SUM
    PROD
    ALL
    ANY
    POLY
    LBOUND
    HBOUND
    DIM

Condition

    ONFILE
    ONLOC
    ONSOURCE
    ONCHAR
    ONKEY
    ONCODE
    DATAFIELD

List processing

    ADDR
    NULL

Others

    DATE
    TIME
    ALLOCATION
    LINENO (filename)
    COUNT (filename)
    ROUND (expression,
      decimal-integer-constant)
    STRING (structure-name)
    EVENT (scalar-event-name)
    PRIORITY (scalar-task-name)

APPENDIX V

C SYNTAX SUMMARY

This summary is aimed mainly to assist in understanding. It is not necessarily a precise statement of the language.

1. Expressions
   The basic expressions are:

   expression:
       primary
       * expression
       & expression
       ~ expression
       ! expression
       - expression
       ++ lvalue
       -- lvalue
       lvalue ++
       lvalue --
       sizeof expression
       (type-name) expression
       expression binop expression
       expression ? expression : expression
       lvalue asgnop expression
       expression, expression

   primary:
       identifier
       constant
       string
       (expression)
       primary (expression-list$_{opt}$)
       primary [expression]
       lvalue . identifier
       primary - identifier

   lvalue:
       identifier
       primary [expression]
       lvalue . identifier
       primary → identifier
       * expression
       (lvalue)

The primary-expression operators

    () [] . →

have highest priority and group left-to-right. The unary operators

    * & - ! ~ ++ -- sizeof (type-name)

have priority over any binary operator but not over any primary operators. The unary operators are grouped right-to-left. The binary and conditional operators, which are all grouped left-to-right, decrease in priority as indicated:

    binop:
        * / %
        + -
        >> <<
        < > <= >=
        == !=
        &
        ^
        |
        &&
        ||
        ?:

Assignment operators, which are all grouped right-to-left, have equal priority.

    asgnop:
        = += -= *= /= %= >>= <<= &= ^= |=

The comma operator groups right-to-left and have lowest priority.

2. Delcarations

   declaration:
       decl-specifiers init-declarator-list$_{opt}$;

   decl-specifiers:
       type-specifier decl-specifiers$_{opt}$
       sc-specifier decl-specifiers$_{opt}$

   sc-specifier:
       auto
       static
       extern
       register
       typedef

   type-specifier:
       char
       short
       int
       long
       unsigned
       float
       double
       struct-or-union-specifier
       typedef-name

   init-declarator-list:
       init-declarator
       init-declarator, init-declarator-list

   init-declarator:
       declarator initializer$_{opt}$

   declarator:
       identifier
       (declarator)
       * declarator
       declarator ()
       declarator [constant-expression$_{opt}$]

struct-or-union-specifier:
  struct (struct-decl-list)
  struct identifier (struct-decl-list)
  struct identifier
  union (struct-decl-list)
  union identifier (struct-decl-list)
  union identifier

struct-decl-list:
  struct-declaration
  struct-declaration struct-decl-list

struct-declaration:
  type-specifier struct-declarator-list;

struct-declarator-list:
  struct-declarator
  struct-declarator, struct-declarator-list

struct-declarator:
  declarator
  declarator : constant-expression
  : constant-expression

initializer:
  = expression
  = (initializer-list)
  = (initializer-list ,)

initializer-list:
  expression
  initializer-list , initializer-list
  (initializer-list)

type-name:
  type-specifier abstract-declarator

abstract-declarator:
  empty
  (abstract-declarator)
  *abstract-declarator
  abstract-declarator ()
  abstract-declarator [constant-expression$_{opt}$]

typedef-name:
  identifier

3. Statements

compound-statement:
  (declaration-list$_{opt}$statement-list$_{opt}$)

declaration-list:
  declaration
  declaration declaration-list

statement-list
  statement
  statement statement-list

statement:
  compound-statement
  expression ;

  if (expression) statement
  if (expression) statement else statement
  while (expression) statement
  do statement while (expression) ;
  for (expression-1$_{opt}$;expression-2$_{opt}$;
    expression-3$_{opt}$) statement
  switch (expression) statement
  case constant-expression : statement
  default : statement
  break ;
  continue ;
  return ;
  return expression ;
  goto identifier ;
  identifier : statement ;

4. External definitions

program:
  external-definition
  external-definition program

external-definition:
  function-definition
  data-definition

function-definition:
  type-specifier$_{opt}$function-declarator
    function-body

function-declarator:
  declarator (parameter-list$_{opt}$)

parameter-list:
  identifier
  identifier , parameter-list

function-body:
  type-decl-list function-statement

function-statement:
  (declaration-list$_{opt}$statement-list)

data definiton:
  extern$_{opt}$type-specifier$_{opt}$init-declarator-list$_{opt}$;
  static$_{opt}$type-specifier$_{opt}$init-declarator-list$_{opt}$;

5. Preprocessor

  #define identifier token-string
  #define identifier (identifier,...,
   identifier) token string
  #undef identifier
  #include "filename"
  #include <filename>
  #if constant-expression
  #ifdef identifier
  #ifndef identifier
  #else
  #endif
  #line constant identifier

APPENDIX VI

PL/1 ARITHMETIC BUILT-IN FUNCTIONS

Function Name and Argument List	Operation	Example
ABS(X)	Produces the absolute value of X	Y = ABS(-14);places 14 in Y.
CEIL(X)	Produces the smallest integer $\geq$ X	Y = CEIL(14.2);places 15 in Y.
FLOOR(X)	Produces the largest integer $\leq$ X	Y = FLOOR(14.2);places 14 in Y.
ROUND(X,n)	Produces the value X rounded to n decimal places	Y = ROUND(14.696,2);places 14.70 in Y.
TRUNC(X)	Produces CEIL(X) if X < 0, FLOOR(X) if X $\geq$ 0	Y = TRUNC(-3.2);places-3 in Y.
		Y = TRUNC(3.2);places 3 in Y.
MAX(X,Y,...,Z)	Produces the largest of the arguments	Y = MAX(12,-20,4,3);places 12 in Y.
MIN(X,Y,...,Z)	Produces the smallest of the arguments	Y = MIN(12,-20,4,3);places -20 in Y.
MOD(X,Y)	Produces a number (integer) equal to the remainder of X/Y	Y = MOD(35,4);places 3 in Y.
EXP(X)	Produces e^X	Y = EXP(3);places 20.086 in Y.
ERF(X)	Produces $\dfrac{2}{\sqrt{\pi}}\displaystyle\int_0^X e^{-t^2}dt$	Y = ERF(1);places .34134 in Y.
ERFC(X)	Produces 1-ERF(X)	Y = ERFC(1);places .65866 in Y.
LOG(X)	Produces $\log_e X$	Y = LOG(2);places .6931 in Y.
LOG10(X)	Produces $\log_{10} X$	Y = LOG10(2);places 0.30103 in Y.
LOG2(X)	Produces $\log_2 X$	Y = LOG2(2);places 1.00000 in Y.
SQRT(X)	Produces $\sqrt{X}$	Y = SQRT(2);places 1.41414 in Y.
SIND(X)	Produces the sine of X, with X representing an angle in degrees	Y = SIND(30);places 0.50000 in Y.
COSD(X)	Produces the cosine of X, with X representing an angle in degrees	Y = COSD(60);places 0.50000 in Y.
SIN(X)	Produces the sine of X, with X representing an angle in radians	Y = sin(0.5236) ;places 0.50000 in Y.
COS(X)	Produces the cosine of X, with X representing an angle in radians	Y = COS(1.0472) ;places 0.50000 in Y.
TAND(X)	Produces the tangent of X, with X representing an angle in degrees	Y = TAND(45);places 1.00000 in Y.
TAN(X)	Produces the tangent of X, with X representing an angle in radians	Y = TAN(.7854);places 1.00000 in Y.
ASIN(X)	Produces $\sin^{-1}X$, expressed in radians	Y = ASIN(0.5);places .5236 in Y.
ACOS(X)	Produces $\cos^{-1}X$, expressed in radians	Y = ACOS(0.5);places 1.0472 in Y.
ATAN(X)	Produces $\tan^{-1}X$, expressed in radians	Y = ATAN(1);places 0.7854 in Y.
ATAND(X)	Produces $\tan^{-1}X$, expressed in degrees	Y = ATAND(1);places 45 in Y.
ATAND(X,Z)	Produces $\tan^{-1}(X/Z)$, expressed in degrees	Y = ATAND(7,7);places 45 in Y.

APPENDIX VII

TABLE OF APL OPERATORS AND LIBRARY FUNCTIONS

NOTE: Some implementations of the language are currently available which provide a software generated APL character set for systems which do not have an APL keyboard. Many implementations will function with the use of "keywords" in place of the APL character set on systems where this is not possible.

Standard scalar operators

Symbol	Syntax	Explanation
+	X + Y	X plus Y
+	+ Y	Y (no change)
-	X - Y	X minus Y
-	- Y	Minus Y
×	X × Y	X times Y
×	× Y	Signum of Y
÷	X ÷ Y	X divided by Y
÷	÷ Y	Reciprocal of Y
*	X * Y	X to the Yth power
*	* Y	e to the Yth power
⌈	X ⌈ Y	Maximum of X and Y
⌈	⌈ Y	Ceiling of Y
⌊	X ⌊ Y	Minimum of X and Y
⌊	⌊ Y	Floor of Y
|	X | Y	X residue of Y
|	| Y	Absolute value of Y
⊛	X ⊛ Y	Log of Y to the base X
⊛	⊛ Y	Natural log of Y
○	○ Y	PI times Y
○	X ○ Y	Trignometric functions and inverses
!	X ! Y	Number of combinations of Y things taken X at a time
!	! Y	Y factorial; Gamma of Y-1
?	? Y	Random equiprobable selection of an integer from Y
<	X < Y	X less than Y
≤	X ≤ Y	X less than or equal to Y
=	X = Y	X equals Y
≥	X ≥ Y	X greater than or equal to Y
>	X > Y	X greater than Y
≠	X ≠ Y	X not equal to Y
∧	X ∧ Y	X and Y
∨	X ∨ Y	X or Y
⍱	X ⍱ Y	Neither X nor Y
⍲	X ⍲ Y	Not both X and Y (X nand Y)
~	~ Y	Not Y

Generalized matrix operations	X+.×Y	Ordinary matrix product of X and Y
	Xψ.ψY	Generalized inner product of X and Y
	Xο.ψY	Generalized outer product of X and Y
Generalized expansion	ψ/Y	The ψ reduction along the last dimension of Y
	ψ/[Z]Y	the ψ reduction along the Zth dimension of Y
Compression and expansion	X/Y	X (logical) compressing along the last dimension of Y
	X/[Z]Y	X (logical) compressing along the Zth dimension of Y
	X\Y	X (logical) expanding along the last dimension of Y
	X\[Z]Y	X (logical) expanding along the Zth dimension of Y
Other Operators	XρY	Reshape Y to the dimensions X
	ρY	The dimension of Y
	X[Y]	The elements of X at locations Y
	XιY	The locations of Y within vector X
	ιY	The first Y consecutive integers (follows index origin)
	XεY	Each element of X is a member of Y
	XτY	Representation of Y in number system X
	X⊥Y	Value of the representation of Y in the number system X
	X?Y	X integers selected without replacement from ιY
	XφY	Rotation by X along the last dimension of Y
	Xφ[Z]Y	Rotation by X along the Zth dimension of Y
	φY	Reversal along the last dimension of Y
	φ[Z]Y	Reversal along the Zth dimension of Y
	X⍉Y	Transpose by X of the coordinates of Y
	⍉Y	Ordinary transpose of Y (transposing last two coordinates only)
	X,Y	Y catenated to X
	,Y	Ravel of Y (make Y a vector)
	X↑Y	Take the first (or last) X elements of Y
	X↓Y	Leave the first (or last) X elements of Y
	X←Y	X specified by Y - the name X receives the value of Y. Value and dimensions of Y are passed on unchanged to the next operator to the the left of X, if any.

	$\not\!\!\!A\, X$	Grade up of X
	$\not\!\!\!\forall X$	Grade down of X
	⊟A	Left inverse of matrix A
	A⊟B	Find X or least squares approximation to X for BX=A where B=matrix coefficients and A=vector of constant terms.

The following special symbols may be used in APL expressions. However, since these symbols do not operate on any function, they are clearly not operators.

Symbols having special functions	( )	Parentheses. Expression within them is to be evaluted before being used as the argument of an operator or defined function.
	→X	Branch to X. Where X is a scalar or a vector, branch to 1ρX. Where X is an empty vector, go to the next line in sequence.
	☐←X	Print the value of X. The value of X is also passed on to the next operator farther to the left.
	X← ☐	Request input. Value of ☐ is the resulting value after expression entered is evaluated.
	X← ⎕	Request input. Value of ⎕ is entire input text as literal characters, up to but not including carrier return.
	'X Y Z'	The literal characters X Y Z.
Trigonmetric and hyperbolic functions Note: t is expressed in radians.	0○t	(1-t*2)*.5
	1○t	sine t
	2○t	cosine t
	3○t	tangent t
	4○t	(1+t*2)*.5
	5○t	sinh t
	6○t	cosh t
	7○t	tanh t
	‾1○t	arcsin t
	‾2○t	arccos t
	‾3○t	arctan t
	‾4○t	(‾1+t*2)*.5
	‾5○t	arcsinh t
	‾6○t	arccosh t
	‾7○t	arctanh t

GLOSSARY

ABSOLUTE ADDRESS—An address that is permanently assigned by the machine designer to a storage location. Synonymous with machine address, specific address.

ABSOLUTE CODING—Coding that uses machine instructions with absolute addresses.

ABSOLUTE ERROR—(1) The amount of error expressed in the same units as the quantity containing the error. (2) Loosely, the absolute value of the error, i.e., the magnitude of the error without regard to its algebraic sign.

ACCESS ARM—A part of a disc storage unit that is used to hold one or more reading and writing heads.

ACCESS TIME—(1) The time interval between the instant at which data are called for from a storage device and the instant delivery begins. (2) The time interval between the instant at which data are requested to be stored and the instant at which storage is started.

ACCUMULATOR—A register in which the result of an arithmetic or logic operation is formed.

ACCURACY—The degree of freedom from error, that is the degree of conformity to truth or to a rule.

ACOUSTIC DELAY LINE—A delay line whose operation is based on the time of propagation of sound waves in a given medium. Synonymous with sonic delay line.

ACOUSTIC MEMORY—Same as acoustic storage.

ACOUSTIC STORAGE—A storage device consisting of acoustic delay lines.

ADDER—A device whose output is a representation of the sum of the quantities represented by its inputs.

ADDRESS—(1) An identification, as represented by a name, label, or number, for a register, location in storage, or any other data source or destination such as the location of a station in a communication network. (2) Loosely, any part of an instruction that specifies the location of an operand for the instruction.

ADDRESS PART—A part of an instruction word that specifies the address of an operand instruction, or result.

ADDRESS REGISTER—A register in which an address is stored.

ADP—Automatic data processing.

ALGOL—ALGOrithmic Language. A language primarily used to express computer programs by algorithms.

ALGORITHM—A prescribed set of well-defined rules or processes for the solution of a problem in a finite number of steps, e.g., a full statement of an arithmetic procedure for evaluating sin x to a stated precision.

ALGORITHMIC LANGUAGE—A language designed for expressing algorithms.

ALPHAMERIC—Same as alphanumeric.

ALPHANUMERIC—Pertaining to a character set that contains letters, digits, and usually other characters such as punctuation marks.

ALPHANUMERIC CHARACTER SET—A character set that contains letters, digits, and usually other characters.

ALPHANUMERIC CODE—A code whose code set consists of letters, digits, and associated special characters.

ANALOG—Pertaining to representation by means of continuously variable physical quantities.

ANALOG COMPUTER—(1) A computer in which analog representation of data is mainly used. (2) A computer that operates on analog data by performing physical processes on these data.

ANALYSIS—The methodical investigation of a problem, and the separation of the problem into smaller related units for further detailed study.

ANALYST—A person who defines problems and develops algorithms and procedures for their solution.

AND—A logic operator having the property that if P is a statement, Q is a statement, R is a statement . . . . , then the AND of P, Q, R . . . , is true if all statements are true, false if any statement is false. P AND Q is often represented by P·Q, PQ. Synonymous with logical multiply.

AND GATE—A gate that implements the logic "AND" operator.

ANNOTATION—An added descriptive comment or explanatory note.

APERTURE—An opening in a data medium or device such as a card or magnetic core; e.g., the aperture in an aperture card combining a microfilm with a punched card or a multiple aperture core.

ARITHMETIC SHIFT—(1) A shift that does not affect the sign position. (2) A shift that is equivalent to the multiplication of a number by a positive or negative integral power of the radix.

ARITHMETIC UNIT—The unit of a computing system that contains the circuits that perform arithmetic operations.

ARRAY—An arrangement of elements in one or more dimensions.

ASSEMBLE—To prepare a machine language program from a symbolic language program by substituting absolute operation codes for symbolic operation codes and absolute or relocatable addresses for symbolic addresses.

ASSEMBLER—A computer program that assembles.

ASSOCIATIVE STORAGE—A storage device in which storage locations are identified by their contents, not by names or positions.

ASYNCHRONOUS COMPUTER—A computer in which each event or the performance of each operation starts as a result of a signal generated by the completion of the previous event or operation, or by the availability of the parts of the computer required for the next event or operation. Contrast with synchronous computer.

AUTOMATIC—Pertaining to a process or device that, under specified conditions, functions without intervention by a human operator.

AUTOMATIC CARRIAGE—A control mechanism for a typewriter or other listing device that can automatically control the feeding, spacing, skipping, and ejecting of paper or preprinted forms.

AUTOMATIC CODING—The machine-assisted preparation of machine language routines.

AUTOMATIC COMPUTER—A computer that can perform a sequence of operations without intervention by a human operator.

AUTOMATIC DATA PROCESSING—Data processing largely performed by automatic means.

AUTOMATION—(1) The implementation of processes by automatic means. (2) The theory, art, or technique of making a process more automatic. (3) The investigation, design, development, and application of methods of rendering processes automatic, self-moving, or self-controlling. (4) The conversion of a procedure, a process, or equipment to automatic operation.

AUXILIARY OPERATION—An offline operation performed by equipment not under control of the central processing unit.

AUXILIARY STORAGE—(1) A storage that supplements another storage. (2) In flowcharting, an offline operation performed by equipment not under control of the central processing unit.

BASE—(1) A reference value. (2) A number that is multiplied by itself as many times as indicated by an exponent. (3) Same as radix. (4) See floating-point base.

BASE ADDRESS—A given address from which an absolute address is derived by combination with a relative address.

BATCH PROCESSING—(1) Pertaining to the technique of executing a set of computer programs such that each is completed before the next program of the set is started. (2)

Pertaining to the sequential input of computer programs or data. (3) Loosely, the execution of computer programs serially.

BAUD—A unit of signalling speed equal to the number of discrete conditions or signal events per second. For example, one baud equals one-half dot cycle per second in Morse code, one bit per second in a train of binary signals, and one 3-bit value per second in a train of signals each of which can assume one of eight different states.

B BOX—Same as index register.

BCD—Binary-coded decimal notation.

BEGINNING-OF-TAPE MARKER—A marker on the magnetic tape used to indicate the beginning of the permissible recording area, e.g., a photo reflective strip, a transparent section of tape.

BINARY—(1) Pertaining to a characteristic or property involving a selection, choice, or condition in which there are two possibilities. (2) Pertaining to the number representation system with a radix of two.

BINARY CODE—A code that makes use of exactly two distinct characters, usually 0 and 1.

BINARY-CODED DECIMAL NOTATION—Positional notation in which the individual decimal digits expressing a number in decimal notation are each represented by a binary numeral. Abbreviated BCD.

BINARY DIGIT—In binary notation, either of the characters, 0 and 1.

BINARY NOTATION—Fixed radix notation where the radix is two.

BIONICS—A branch of technology relating the functions, characteristics, and phenomena of living systems to the development of hardware systems.

BIQUINARY CODE—A mixed radix notation in which each decimal digit to be represented is considered as a sum of two digits of which the first is zero or one with a significance five and the second is 0, 1, 2, 3, or 4 with significance one.

BISTABLE—Pertaining to a device capable of assuming either one of two stable states.

BIT—A binary digit.

BIT STRING—A string of binary digits in which the position of each binary digit is considered as an independent unit.

BLOCK DIAGRAM—A diagram of a system, instrument, or computer in which the principal parts are represented suitably associated geometrical figures to show both the basic functions and the function relationships among the parts.

BLOCK TRANSFER—The process of transmitting one or more blocks of data where the data are organized in blocks.

BOOLEAN—(1) Pertaining to the processes used in the algebra formulated by George Boole. (2) Pertaining to the operations of formal logic.

BOOLEAN ADD—Same as OR.

BOOLEAN OPERATOR—A logic operator each of whose operands and whose result have one of two values.

BOOTSTRAP—A technique or device designed to bring itself into a desired state by means of its own action e.g., a machine routine whose first few instructions are sufficient to bring the rest of itself into the computer from an input device.

BORROW—An arithmetically negative carry.

BRANCH—(1) A set of instructions that are executed between two successive decision instructions. (2) Loosely, a conditional jump.

BRANCHPOINT—A place in a routine where a branch is selected.

BREAKPOINT—A place in a routine specified by an instruction digit, or other condition, where the routine may be interrupted by external intervention or by a monitor routine.

BUFFER—(1) A routine or storage used to compensate for a difference in rate of flow of data, or time of occurrence of events, when transmitting data from one device to another. (2) An isolating circuit used to prevent a driven circuit from influencing the driving circuit.

BUG—A mistake or malfunction.

BURST—(1) To separate continuous-form paper into discrete sheets. (2) In data transmission, a sequence of signals counted as one unit in accordance with some specific criterion or measure.

BUS—One or more conductors used for transmitting signals or power.

BYTE—A sequence of adjacent binary digits operated upon as a unit and usually shorter than a computer word.

CALCULATOR—(1) A data processor especially suitable for performing arithmetical operations which require frequent intervention by a human operator. (2) Generally and historically, a device for carrying out logic and arithmetic digital operations of any kind.

CALL—To transfer control to a specified close subroutine.

CALLING SEQUENCE—A specified arrangement of instructions and data necessary to set up and call a given subroutine.

CAPACITOR STORAGE—A storage device that utilizes the capacitance properties of materials to store data.

CARD COLUMN—A single line of punch positions parallel to the short edge of a 3 1/4 by 7 3/8 inch punched card.

CARD DECK—Same as deck.

CARD HOPPER—The portion of a card processing machine that holds the cards to be processed and makes them available to a card feed mechanism.

CARD IMAGE—A one-to-one representation of the hole patterns of a punched card, e.g., a matrix in which a one represents a punch and zero represents the absence of a punch.

CARD ROW—A single line of punch positions parallel to the long edge of a 3 1/4 by 7 3/8 inch punched card.

CARD STACKER—The portion of a card processing machine that receives processed cards.

CARRIAGE CONTROL TAPE—A tape that contains line feed control data for a printing device.

CARRIAGE RETURN—The operation that prepares for the next character to be printed or displayed at the specified first position on the same line.

CARRY—(1) One or more digits, produced in connection with an arithmetic operation on one digit place of two or more numerals in positional notation, that are forwarded to another digit place for processing there. (2) The number represented by the digit or digits in (1). (3) Most commonly, a digit as defined in (1), that arises when the sum or product of two or more digits equals or exceeds the radix of the number representation system.

CASCADED CARRY—In parallel addition, a carry process in which the addition of two numerals results in a partial sum numeral and a carry numeral which are in turn added together, this process being repeated until no new carries are generated.

CATHODE RAY STORAGE—An electrostatic storage device that utilizes a cathode ray beam for access to the data.

CENTRAL PROCESSING UNIT—A unit of a computer that includes the circuits controlling the interpretation and execution of instructions. Synonymous with main frame. Abbreviated CPU.

CENTRAL PROCESSOR—A central processing unit.

CHAD—The piece of material removed when forming a hole or notch in a storage medium such as punched tape or punched cards. Synonymous with chip.

CHADLESS—Pertaining to the punching of tape in which chad does not result.

CHAIN PRINTER—A printer in which the type slugs are carried by the links of a revolving chain.

CHANGE DUMP—A selective dump of those storage locations whose contents have changed.

CHANNEL—(1) A path along which signals can be sent, e.g., data channel, output channel. (2) The portion of a storage medium that is accessible to a given reading or writing station, e.g., track, band.

CHARACTER—(1) A letter, digit, or other symbol that is used as part of the organization, control, or representation of data. A character is often in the form of a spatial arrangement of adjacent or connected strokes.

CHARACTER CHECK—A check that verifies the observance of rules for the formation of characters.

CHARACTER PRINTER—A device that prints a single character at a time.

CHARACTER RECOGNITION—The identification of graphic, phonic, or other characters by automatic means.

CHARACTER SET—A set of unique representations called characters e.g., the 26 letters of the English alphabet, 0 and 1 of the Boolean alphabet, and the set of signals in the Morse code alphabet.

CHARACTER STRING—A string consisting solely of characters.

CHARACTER SUBSET—A selection of characters from a character set, comprising all characters which have a specified common feature. For example, in the definition of character set, digits 0 through 9 constitute a character subset.

CHECK—A process for determining accuracy.

CLEAR—To place one or more storage locations into a prescribed state, usually zero or the space character.

CLOCK—(1) A device that generates periodic signals used for synchronization. (2) A register whose content changes at regular intervals in such a way as to measure time.

CLOCK PULSE—A synchronization signal provided by a clock.

CLOCK TRACK—A track on which a pattern of signals has been recorded to provide a time reference.

CLOSED SUBROUTINE—A subroutine that can be stored at one place and can be linked to one or more calling routines.

COBOL—(COmmon Business Oriented Language) A business data processing language.

CODE—In data processing, to represent data or a computer program in a symbolic form that can be accepted by a data processor.

CODER—A person mainly involved in writing but not designing computer programs.

COLLATE—To combine items from two or more ordered sets into one set having a specified order not necessarily the same as any of the original sets.

COLLATING SEQUENCE—An ordering assigned to a set of items, such that any two sets in that assigned order can be collated.

COLLATOR—A device to collate, merge, or match sets of punched cards or other documents.

COLUMN—(1) A vertical arrangement of characters or other expressions. (2) Loosely, a digit place.

COMMAND—(1) A control signal. (2) Loosely, an instruction in machine language.

COMMAND LANGUAGE—A source language consisting primarily of procedural operators, each capable of invoking a function to be executed.

COMMON FIELD—A field that can be accessed by two or more independent routines.

COMMUNICATION LINK—The physical means of connecting one location to another for the purpose of transmitting and receiving data.

COMPILE—To prepare a machine language program from a computer program written in another programming language by making use of the overall logic structure of the program, or generating more than one machine instruction for each symbolic statement, or both, as well as performing the function of an assembler.

COMPILER—A program that compiles.

COMPLEMENT—(1) A number that can be derived from a specified number by subtracting it from a second specified number. For example, in radix notation, the second specified number may be a given power of the radix or one less than a given power of the radix. The negative of a number is often represented by its complement.

COMPLETE CARRY—In parallel addition, a technique in which all of the carries are allowed to propagate.

COMPUTER—A data processor that can perform substantial computation, including numerous arithmetic or logic operations, without intervention by a human operator during the run.

COMPUTER CODE—A machine code for a specific computer.

COMPUTER INSTRUCTION—A machine instruction for a specific computer.

COMPUTER NETWORK—A complex consisting of two or more interconnected computers.

COMPUTER PROGRAM—A series of instructions or statements, in a form acceptable to a computer, prepared in order to achieve a certain result.

COMPUTER WORD—A sequence of bits or characters treated as a unit and capable of being stored in one computer location. Synonymous with machine word.

CONCURRENT—Pertaining to the occurrence of two or more events or activities within the same specified interval of time.

CONDITIONAL JUMP—A jump that occurs if specified criteria are met.

CONNECTOR—(1) On a flowchart, the means of representing the convergence of more than one flowline into one, or the divergence of one flowline into more than one. It may also represent a break in a single flowline for continuation in another area. (2) A means of representing on a flowchart a break in a line of flow.

CONSECUTIVE—Pertaining to the occurrence of two sequential events without the intervention of any other such event.

CONSOLE—That part of a computer used for communication between the operator or maintenance engineer and the computer.

CONTRAST—In optical character recognition, the differences between color or shading of the printed material on a document and the background on which it is printed.

CONTROL PANEL—A part of a computer console that contains manual controls.

CONVERT—To change the representation of data from one form to another, e.g., to change numerical data from binary to decimal or from cards to tape.

COPY—To reproduce data in a new location or other destination, leaving the source data unchanged, although the physical form of the result may differ from that of the source. For example, to copy a deck of cards onto a magnetic tape. Contrast with duplicate.

CORRECTIVE MAINTENANCE—Maintenance specifically intended to eliminate an existing fault.

CORRECTIVE MAINTENANCE TIME—Time, either scheduled or unscheduled, used to perform corrective maintenance.

COUNTER—A device such as a register or storage location used to represent the number of occurrences of an event.

CPU—Central Processing Unit.

CROSSTALK—The unwanted energy transferred from one circuit, called the "disturbing" circuit, to another circuit, called the "disturbed" circuit.

CRT DISPLAY—Cathode Ray Tube display.

CYBERNETICS—That branch of learning which brings together theories and studies on communication and control in living organisms and machines.

CYCLE—(1) An interval of space or time in which one set of events or phenomena is completed. (2) Any set of operations that is repeated regularly in the same sequence. The operations may be subject to variations on each repetition.

CYCLIC SHIFT—A shift in which the data moved out of one end of the storing register are reentered into the other end, as in a closed loop.

DATA—(1) A representation of facts, concepts, or instructions in a formalized manner suitable for communication, interpretation, or processing by humans or automatic means. (2) Any representations such as characters or analog quantities to which meaning is or might be assigned.

DATA BANK—A comprehensive collection of libraries of data.

DATA FLOW CHART—A flowchart representing the path of data through a problem solution. It defines the major phases of the processing as well as the various data media used.

DATA HIERARCHY—A data structure consisting of sets and subsets such that every subset of a set is of lower rank than the data of the set.

DATA MEDIUM—(1) The material in or on which a specific physical variable may represent data. (2) The physical quantity which may be varied to represent data.

DATA PROCESSING—The execution of a sys-tematic sequence of operations performed upon data. Synonymous with information processing.

DATA PROCESSOR—A device capable of performing data processing, including desk calculators, punched card machines, and computers.

DATA REDUCTION—The transformation of raw data into a more useful form.

DEBUG—To detect, locate, and remove mistakes from a routine or malfunctions from a computer. Synonymous with troubleshoot.

DECIMAL—Pertaining to the number representation system with a radix of ten.

DECIMAL DIGIT—In decimal notation, one of the characters 0 through 9.

DECIMAL NOTATION—A fixed radix notation where the radix is ten.

DECIMAL NUMERAL—A decimal representation of a number.

DECIMAL POINT—The radix point in decimal representation.

DECISION—A determination of future action.

DECISION INSTRUCTION—An instruction that effects the selection of a branch of a program, e.g., a conditional jump instruction.

DECK—A collection of punched cards. Synonymous with card deck.

DECODE—To apply a set of unambiguous rules specifying the way in which data may be restored to a previous representation.

DECODER—(1) A device that decodes. (2) A matrix of logic elements that selects one or more output channels according to the combination of input signals present.

DECOLLATE—To separate the plies of a multipart form or paper stock.

DEFERRED MAINTENANCE—Maintenance specifically intended to eliminate an existing fault, which did not prevent continued successful operation of the device or program.

DELAY—The amount of time by which an event is retarded.

DELEAVE—Same as decollate.

DELIMITER—A flag that separates and organizes items of data. Synonymous with separator.

DESCRIPTOR—In information retrieval, a word used to categorize or index information. Synonymous with keyword.

DESTRUCTIVE READ—A read process that also erases the data from the source.

DEVELOPMENT TIME—That part of operating time used for debugging new routines or hardware.

DIAGNOSTIC—Pertaining to the detection and isolation of a malfunction or mistake.

DIGIT—A symbol that represents one of the positive integers smaller than the radix.

DIGITAL—Pertaining to data in the form of digits.

DIGITAL COMPUTER—(1) A computer in which discrete representation of data is mainly used. (2) A computer that operates on discrete data by performing arithmetic and logic processes on these data.

DIGITIZE—To use numeric characters to express or represent data.

DIGIT PUNCH—A punch in rows 1, 2, . . . , 9 of a punched card.

DIMINISHED RADIX COMPLEMENT—Same as radix-minus-one complement.

DIRECT ACCESS—(1) Pertaining to the process of obtaining data from, or placing data into, storage where the time required for such access is independent of the location of the data most recently obtained or placed in storage. (2) Pertaining to a storage device in which the access time is effectively independent of the location of the data. (3) Synonymous with random access (1).

DIRECT ADDRESS—An address that specifies the location of an operand.

DISASTER DUMP—A dump made when a nonrecoverable program error occurs.

DISCRETE—Pertaining to distinct elements or to representation by means of distinct elements such as characters.

DISPLAY—A visual presentation of data.

DOCUMENT—(1) A medium and the data recorded on it for human use. (2) By extension, any record that has permanence and that can be read by man or machine.

DOCUMENT REFERENCE EDGE—In character recognition, a specified document edge with respect to which the alignment of characters is defined.

DOCUMENTATION—(1) The creating, collecting, organizing, storing, citing, and disseminating of documents or the information recorded in documents. (2) A collection of documents or information on a given subject.

DOUBLE PRECISION—Pertaining to the use of two computer words to represent a number.

DOWNTIME—The time interval during which a device is malfunctioning.

DROP OUT—(1) In magnetic tape, a recorded signal whose amplitude is less than a predetermined percentage of a reference signal. (2) In data transmission, a momentary loss in signal, usually due to the effect of noise or system malfunction.

DUMP—(1) To copy the contents of all or part of a storage, usually from an internal storage into an external storage. (2) A process as in (1). (3) The data resulting from the process as in (1).

DUODECIMAL—(1) Pertaining to a characteristic or property involving a selection, choice, or condition in which there are twelve possibilities. (2) Pertaining to the numeration system with a radix of twelve.

DUPLICATE—To copy so that the result remains in the same physical form as the source, e.g., to make a new punched card with the same pattern of holes as an original punched card. Contrast with copy.

DYNAMIC DUMP—A dump that is performed during the execution of a computer program.

DYNAMIC STORAGE—A device storing data in a manner that permits the data to move or vary with time such that the specified data are not always available for recovery. Magnetic-drum and disc storage are nonvolatile dynamic storage. An acoustic delay line is a volatile dynamic storage.

DYNAMIC STORAGE ALLOCATION—A storage allocation technique in which the location of computer programs and data is determined by criteria applied at the moment of need.

EAM—Electrical Accounting Machine.

EDIT—To modify the form or format of data, e.g., to insert or delete characters such as page numbers or decimal points.

EDP—Electronic Data Processing.

ELECTRONIC DATA PROCESSING—(1) Data processing largely performed by electronic devices. (2) Pertaining to data processing equipment that is predominantly electronic such as an electronic digital computer.

ELECTROSTATIC STORAGE—A storage device that stores data as electrostatically charged areas on a dielectric surface.

ELEVEN-PUNCH—A punch in the second row from the top, on a Hollerith punched card. Synonymous with x-punch.

EMERGENCY MAINTENANCE—Maintenance specifically intended to eliminate an existing fault, which makes continued production work unachievable.

EMERGENCY MAINTENANCE TIME—Time, usually unscheduled, used to perform corrective maintenance.

ENCODE—To apply a set of unambiguous rules specifying the way in which data may be represented such that a subsequent decoding is possible.

END-AROUND CARRY—A carry from the most significant digit place to the least significant place.

END-OF-TAPE MARKER—A marker on a magnetic tape used to indicate the end of the permissible recording area, e.g., a photo reflective strip, a transparent section of tape, a particular bit pattern.

ENTRY CONDITIONS—The initial data and control conditions to be satisfied for successful execution of a given routine.

ENTRY POINT—In a routine, any place to which control can be passed.

ERASE—To obliterate information from a storage medium, e.g., to clear, to overwrite.

ERROR—Any discrepancy between a computed, observed, or measured quantity and the true, specified, or theoretically correct value or condition.

ERROR DETECTING CODE—A code in which each expression conforms to specific rules of construction, so that if certain errors occur in an expression the resulting expression will not conform to the rules of construction and, thus, the presence of the errors is detected. Synonymous with self-checking code.

ERROR MESSAGE—An indication that an error has been detected.

ERROR RANGE—The difference between the highest and lowest error values.

ERROR RATIO—The ratio of the number of data units in error to the total number of data units.

EXCESS THREE CODE—A binary coded decimal notation in which each decimal digit

N is represented by the binary numeral of N plus three.

EXCLUSIVE OR—A logic operator having the property that if P is a statement and Q is a statement, then P exclusive OR Q is true if either but not both statements are true, false if both are true or both are false. P exclusive OR Q is often represented by $P \oplus Q$, $P \veebar Q$. Contrast with OR.

EXECUTIVE ROUTINE—A routine that controls the execution of other routines.

EXPONENT—In a floating point representation, the numeral, of a pair of numerals representing a number, that indicates the power to which the base is raised.

FALSE ADD—To form a partial sum, i.e., to add without carries.

FAULT—(1) A physical condition that causes a device, a component, or an element to fail to perform in a required manner, e.g., a short circuit, a broken wire, an intermittent connection.

FEEDBACK LOOP—The components and processes involved in correcting or controlling a system by using part of the output as input.

FERRITE—An iron compound frequently used in the construction of magnetic cores.

FIELD—In a record, a specified area used for a particular category of data, e.g., a group of card columns used to represent a wage rate, a set of bit locations in a computer word used to express the address of the operand.

FILE—A collection of related records treated as a unit.

FILE GAP—An area on a data medium intended to be used to indicate the end of a file, and possibly, the start of another. A file gap is frequently used for other purposes, in particular, as a flag to indicate the end or beginning of some other group of data.

FILE LAYOUT—The arrangement and structure of data in a file, including the sequence and size of its components. By extension, a file layout might be the description thereof.

FILE MAINTENANCE—The activity of keeping a file up to date by adding, changing or deleting data.

FILE SEPARATOR—The information separator intended to identify a logical boundary between items called "files." Abbreviated FS.

FILTER—(1) A device or program that separates data, signals, or material in accordance with specified criteria. (2) A mask.

FIXED-CYCLE OPERATION—An operation that is completed in a specified number of regularly timed execution cycles.

FIXED-POINT PART—In a floating-point representation, the numeral of a pair of numerals representing a number, that is the fixed-point factor by which the power is multiplied.

FIXED-POINT REPRESENTATION—A positional representation in which each number is represented by a single set of digits, the position of the radix point being fixed with respect to one end of the set, according to some convention.

FIXED RADIX NOTATION—A positional representation in which the significances of successive digit positions are successive integral power of a single radix. When the radix is positive, permissible values of each digit range from zero to one less than the radix, and negative integral powers of the radix are used to represent fractions.

FIXED STORAGE—Storage whose contents are not alterable by computer instructions, e.g., magnetic core storage with a lockout feature, photographic disc. Synonymous with nonerasable storage, permanent storage, read-only storage.

FLAG—(1) Any of various types of indicators used for identification, e.g., a wordmark. (2) A character that signals the occurrence of some condition, such as the end of a word. (3) Synonymous with mark, sentinel, tag.

FLIP-FLOP—A circuit or device containing

active elements, capable of assuming either one of two stable states at a given time. Synonymous with toggle.

FLOATING-POINT BASE—In floating point representation, the fixed positive integer that is the base of the power. Synonymous with floating-point radix.

FLOATING-POINT REPRESENTATION—A number representation system in which each number as represented by a pair of numerals equals one of those numerals times a power of an implicit fixed positive integer base where the power is equal to the implicit base raised to the exponent represented by the other numeral.

Common Notation

0.0001234 or $(O.1234) \times (10^{-3})$

A Floating Representation

1234 - 03

FLOWCHART—A graphical representation for the definition, analysis, or solution of a problem, in which symbols are used to represent operations, data, flow, equipment, etc.

FLOWCHART SYMBOL—A symbol used to represent operations, data, flow, or equipment on a flowchart.

FLOWCHART TEXT—The descriptive information that is associated with flowchart symbols.

FLOW DIRECTION—In flowcharting, the antecedent-to-successor relation, indicated by arrows or other conventions, between operations on a flowchart.

FLOWLINE—On a flowchart, a line representing a connecting path between flowchart symbols.

FORMAT—The arrangement of data.

FORTRAN—(FORmula TRANSlating system) A language primarily used to express computer

programs by arithmetic formulas.

FRAME—An area, one recording position long, extending across the width of a magnetic or paper tape perpendicular to its movement. Several bits or punch positions may be included in a single frame through the use of different recording positions across the width of the tape.

FUNCTION—A specific purpose of an entity, or its characteristic action.

FUNCTIONAL DESIGN—The specification of the working relations between the parts of a system in terms of their characteristic actions.

FUNCTIONAL DIAGRAM—A diagram that represents the functional relationships among the parts of a system.

GATE—A device having one output channel and one or more input channels, such as the output channel state is completely determined by the input channel states, except during switching transients, e.g., AND GATE; OR GATE.

GENERAL PURPOSE COMPUTER—A computer that is designed to handle a wide variety of problems.

GRAY CODE—A binary code in which sequential numbers are represented by binary expressions, each of which differs from the preceding expression in one place only. Synonymous with reflected binary code.

HALF-ADDER—A combinational logic element having two outputs. S and C, and two inputs, A and B, such that the outputs are related to the inputs according to the following table.

input		output	
A	B	C	S
0	0	0	0
0	1	0	1
1	0	0	1
1	1	1	0

S denotes "Sum Without Carry," C denotes "Carry." Two half-adders may be used for performing binary addition.

HALF-WORD—A contiguous sequence of bits or characters which comprises half a computer word and is capable of being addressed as a unit.

HAMMING CODE—A data code which is capable of being corrected automatically.

HARDWARE—Physical equipment, as opposed to the computer program or method of use, e.g., mechanical, magnetic, electrical, or electronic devices. Contrast with software.

HEAD—A device that reads, writes, or erases data on a storage medium, e.g., a small electromagnet used to read, write, or erase data on a magnetic drum or tape, or the set of perforating, reading, or marking devices used for punching, reading, or printing on paper tape.

HEADER CARD—A card that contains information related to the data in cards that follow.

HEXADECIMAL—Same as sexadecimal.

HIERARCHY—See data hierarchy.

HIGH-SPEED CARRY—Any technique in parallel addition for speeding up carry propagation.

HIT—A successful comparison of two items of data.

HOLE PATTERN—A punching configuration within a card column that represents a single character of a character set.

HOLLERITH—Pertaining to a particular type of code or punched card utilizing 12 rows per column and usually 80 columns per card.

HYBRID COMPUTER—A computer for data processing using both analog representation and discrete representation of data.

IDENTIFIER—A symbol whose purpose is to identify, indicate, or name a body of data.

IDLE TIME—That part of available time during which the hardware is not being used.

IDP—See Integrated Data Processing.

ILLEGAL CHARACTER—A character or combination of bits that is not valid according to some criteria, e.g., with respect to a specified alphabet a character that is not a member.

INCONNECTOR—In flowcharting, a connector that indicates a continuation of a broken flowline.

INDEX REGISTER—A register whose content may be added to or subtracted from the operand address prior to or during the execution of a ·computer instruction. Synonymous with B box.

INFORMATION—The meaning that a human assigns to data by means of the known conventions used in their representation.

INFORMATION PROCESSING— Same as data processing.

INFORMATION RETRIEVAL—The methods and procedures for recovering specific information from stored data.

INHERITED ERROR—An error carried forward from a previous step in a sequential process.

INHIBITING SIGNAL—A signal that prevents an operation from taking place.

INITIALIZE—To set counters, switches, and addresses to zero or other starting values at the beginning of, or at prescribed points in, a computer routine. Synonymous with prestore.

INPUT—Pertaining to a device process, or channel involved in the insertion of data or states, or to the data or states involved.

INPUT AREA—An area of storage reserved for input.

INPUT CHANNEL—A channel for impressing a state on a device or logic element.

INPUT DATA—Data to be processed.

INPUT DEVICE—The device or collective set of

devices used for conveying data into another device.

INPUT/OUTPUT—Pertaining to either input or output, or both.

INSTALLATION TIME—Time spent in installing and testing either hardware, or software, or both, until they are accepted.

INSTRUCTION—A statement that specifies an operation and the values or locations of its operands.

INSTRUCTION ADDRESS—The address that must be used to fetch an instruction.

INSTRUCTION COUNTER—A counter that indicates the location of the next computer instruction to be interpreted.

INSTRUCTION REGISTER—A register that stores an instruction for execution.

INSTRUCTION REPERTOIRE—The set of operations that can be represented in a given operation code.

INTEGRATED DATA PROCESSING—Data processing in which the coordination of data acquisition and all other stages of data processing is achieved in a coherent system, e.g., a business data processing system in which data for orders and buying are combined to accomplish the functions of scheduling, invoicing, and accounting. Abbreviated IDP.

INTERFACE—A shared boundary. An interface might be a hardware component to link two devices or it might be a portion of storage or registers accessed by two or more computer programs.

INTERLEAVE—To arrange parts of one sequence of things or events so that they alternate with parts of one or more other sequences of things or events and so that each sequence retains its identity, e.g., to organize storage into banks with independent bases so that sequential data references may be overlapped in a given period of time.

INTERNAL STORAGE—Addressable storage directly controlled by the central processing unit of a digital computer.

INTERPRETER—(1) A computer program that translates and executes each source language statement before translating and executing the next one. (2) A device that prints on a punched card the data already punched in the card.

INTERRUPT—To stop a process in such a way that it can be resumed.

INVERT—To change a physical or logical state to its opposite.

I/O—An abbreviation for input/output.

ITEM—(1) In general, one member of a group, e.g., a record may contain a number of items such as fields or groups of fields: a file may consist of a number of items such as records; a table may consist of a number of items such as entries. (2) A collection of related characters, treated as a unit.

JOB—A specified group of tasks prescribed as a unit of work for a computer.

JUMP—A departure from the normal sequence of executing instructions in a computer. Synonymous with transfer.

JUSTIFY—(1) To adjust the printing positions of characters on a page so that the lines have the desired length and that both the left and right hand margins are regular. (2) By extension, to shift the contents of a register so that the most or the least significant digit is at some specified position in the register.

K—An abbreviation for the prefix kilo, i.e., 1000 in decimal notation.

KEYPUNCH—A keyboard actuated device that punches holes in a card to represent data.

LABEL—One or more characters used to identify a statement or an item of data in a computer program.

LACED CARD—A punched card that has a

lace-like appearance, usually without information content.

LAG—The delay between two events.

LANGUAGE—A set of representations, conventions, and rules used to convey information.

LEADER—The blank section of tape at the beginning of a reel of tape.

LEFT-JUSTIFY—(1) To adjust the printing positions of characters on a page so that the left margin of the page is regular. (2) By extension, to shift the contents of a register so that the most significant digit is at some specified position of the register.

LEVEL—The degree of subordination in a hierarchy.

LIBRARY—(1) A collection of organized information used for study and reference. (2) A collection of related files.

LIBRARY ROUTINE—A proven routine that is maintained in a program library.

LINE PRINTER—A device that prints all characters of a line as a unit.

LINE PRINTING—The printing of an entire line of characters as a unit.

LINKAGE—In programming, coding that connects two separately coded routines.

LIST—An ordered set of items.

LOAD—In programming, to enter data into storage or working registers.

LOAD-AND-GO—An operating technique in which there are no stops between the loading and execution phases of a program, and which may include assembling or compiling.

LOCATION—Any place in which data may be stored.

LOGICAL FILE—A collection of one or more logical records.

LOGIC ELEMENT—A device that performs a logic function.

LOGIC INSTRUCTION—An instruction that executes an operation that is defined in symbolic logic, such as AND, OR, NOR.

LOGIC SHIFT—A shift that affects all positions.

LOGIC SYMBOL—(1) A symbol used to represent a logic element graphically. (2) A symbol used to represent a logic operator.

LOOP—A sequence of instructions that is executed repeatedly until a terminal condition prevails.

MACHINE CODE—An operation code that a machine is designed to recognize.

MACHINE INSTRUCTION—An instruction that a machine can recognize and execute.

MACHINE LANGUAGE—A language that is used directly by a machine.

MACHINE WORD—Same as computer word.

MACRO INSTRUCTION—An instruction in a source language that is equivalent to a specified sequence of machine instructions.

MACROPROGRAMMING—Programming with macro instructions.

MAGNETIC CARD—A card with a magnetic surface on which data can be stored by selective magnetization of portions of the flat surface.

MAGNETIC CORE—A configuration of magnetic material that is, or is intended to be, placed in a spatial relationship to current-carrying conductors and whose magnetic properties are essential to its use. It may be used to concentrate an induced magnetic field as in a transformer induction coil, or armature, to retain a magnetic polarization for the purpose of storing data, or for its nonlinear properties as in a logic element. It may be made of such material as iron, iron oxide, or ferrite and in such shapes as wires, tapes, toroids, rods, or thin film.

MAGNETIC DELAY LINE—A delay line whose operation is based on the time of propagation of magnetic waves.

MAGNETIC DISC—A flat circular plate with a magnetic surface on which data can be stored by selective magnetization of portions of the flat surface.

MAGNETIC DRUM—A right circular cylinder with a magnetic surface on which data can be stored by selective magnetization of portions of the curved surface.

MAGNETIC HYSTERESIS LOOP—A closed curve showing the relation between the magnetization force and the induction of magnetization in a magnetic substance when the magnetized field (force) is carried through a complete cycle.

MAGNETIC INK—An ink that contains particles of a magnetic substance whose presence can be detected by magnetic sensors.

MAGNETIC STORAGE—A storage device that utilizes the magnetic properties of materials to store data, e.g., magnetic cores, tapes, and films.

MAGNETIC TAPE—(1) A tape with a magnetic surface on which data can be stored by selective polarization of portions of the surface. (2) A tape of magnetic material used as the constituent in some forms of magnetic cores.

MAGNETIC THIN FILM—A layer of magnetic material, usually less than one micron thick, often used for logic or storage elements.

MAIN FRAME—Same as central processing unit.

MAIN STORAGE—The general-purpose storage of a computer. Usually, main storage can be accessed directly by the operating registers.

MAINTENANCE—Any activity intended to eliminate faults or to keep hardware or programs in satisfactory working condition, including tests, measurements, replacements, adjustments, and repairs.

MAINTENANCE TIME—Time used for hardware maintenance. It includes preventive maintenance time and corrective maintenance time.

MANTISSA—The fractional part of a logarithm.

MARGINAL CHECK—A preventive maintenance procedure in which certain operating conditions, such as supply voltage or frequency, are varied about their nominal values in order to detect and locate incipiently defective parts.

MARK—Same as flag.

MASS STORAGE DEVICE—A device having a large storage capacity, e.g., magnetic disc, magnetic drum.

MASTER FILE—A file that is either relatively permanent, or that is treated as an authority in a particular job.

MATCH—To check for identity between two or more items of data.

MATHEMATICAL MODEL—A mathematical representation of a process, device, or concept.

MATRIX—(1) In mathematics, a two-dimensional rectangular array of quantities. Matrices are manipulated in accordance with the rules of matrix algebra. (2) In computers, a logic network in the form of an array of input leads and output leads with logic elements connected at some of their intersections. (3) By extension, an array of any number of dimensions.

MATRIX STORAGE—Storage, the elements of which are arranged such that access to any location requires the use of two or more coordinates, e.g., cathode ray storage, magnetic core storage.

MEDIUM—The material, or configuration thereof, on which data are recorded, e.g., paper tape, cards, magnetic tape. Synonymous with data medium.

MEMORY—Same as storage.

MERGE—To combine items from two or more similarly ordered sets into one set that is arranged in the same order. Contrast with collate.

MESSAGE—An arbitrary amount of information whose beginning and end are defined or implied.

MISTAKE—A human action that produces an unintended result.

MNEMONIC SYMBOL—A symbol chosen to assist the human memory, e.g., an abbreviation such as "mpy" for "multiply."

MODEM—(MOdulator-DEModulator) A device that modulates signals transmitted over communication facilities.

MODULE—(1) A program unit that is discrete and identifiable with respect to compiling, combining with other units, and loading, e.g., the input to, or output from, an assembler, compiler, linkage editor, or executive routine. (2) A packaged functional hardware unit designed for use with other components.

MONITOR—Software or hardware that observes, supervises, controls, or verifies the operations of a system.

MONOSTABLE—Pertaining to a device that has one stable state.

MULTIPLE PUNCHING—Punching more than one hole in the same column of a punched card by means of more than one keystroke.

MULTIPLEX—To interleave or simultaneously transmit two or more messages on a single channel.

MULTIPROCESSING—Pertaining to the simultaneous execution of two or more computer programs or sequences of instructions by a computer or computer network.

MULTIPROCESSOR—A computer employing two or more processing units under integrated control.

MULTIPROGRAMMING—Pertaining to the concurrent execution of two or more programs by a computer.

NAND—A logic operator having the property that if P is a statement, Q is a statement, R is a statement. . . , then the NAND OF P, Q, R . . . is true if at least one statement is false, false if all statements are true. Synonymous with NOT-AND.

NATURAL LANGUAGE—A language whose rules reflect and describe current usage rather than prescribe usage.

N-CORE-PER-BIT STORAGE—A storage device that employs n magnetic cores for each bit to be stored.

NDR—See nondestructive read.

NEGATE—To perform the logic operation NOT.

NEST—To imbed subroutines or data in other subroutines of data at a different hierarchical level such that the different levels of routines or data can be executed or accessed recursively.

NOISE—(1) Random variations of one or more characteristics of any entity such as voltage, current, or data. (2) A random signal of known statistical properties of amplitude, distribution and spectral density. (3) Loosely, any disturbance tending to interfere with the normal operation of a device or system.

NONDESTRUCTIVE READ—A read process that does not erase the data in the source. Abbreviated NDR.

NON-RETURN-TO-ZERO (MARK) RECORDING—A method of recording in which ones are represented by a change in the condition of magnetization; zeros are represented by the absence of change. Abbreviated NRZ(M).

NON-RETURN-TO-ZERO RECORDING—A method of recording in which the change between the state of magnetization representing either zero or one provides the reference condition. Synonymous with non-return-to-reference recording. Abbreviated NRZ.

NO-OP–An instruction that specifically instructs the computer to do nothing, except to proceed to the next instruction in sequence.

NOR–A logic operator having the property that if P is a statement, Q is a statement, R is a statement . . . , then the NOR of P, Q, R . . . is true if all statements are false, false if at least one statement is true. P NOR Q is often represented by a combination of "OR" and "NOT" symbols, such as ~ (PVQ). P NOR Q is also called "neither P nor Q." Synonymous with NOT-OR.

NORMAL DIRECTION FLOW–A flow in a direction from left to right or top to bottom on a flowchart.

NORMALIZE–(1) To multiply a variable or one or more quantities occurring in a calculation by a numerical coefficient in order to make an associated quantity assume a nominated value, e.g., to make a definite integral of a variable, or the maximum member of a set of quantities, equal to unity. (2) Loosely, a scale.

NOT–A logic operator having the property that if P is a statement, then the NOT of P is true if P is false, false if P is true. The NOT of P is often represented by $\bar{P}$, ~P, $\daleth$P, P'.

NOT-AND–Same as NAND.

NOT-OR–Same as NOR.

NRZ–Non-Return-to-Zero recording.

NRZ(M)–Non-Return-to-Zero (Mark) recording.

NUMBER–(1) A mathematical entity that may indicate quantity or amount of units. (2) Loosely, a numeral.

NUMBER REPRESENTATION–The representation of numbers by agreed sets of symbols according to agreed rules. Synonymous with numeration.

NUMBER REPRESENTATION SYSTEM–An agreed set of symbols and rules for number representation.

NUMBER SYSTEM–Loosely, a number representation system.

NUMERAL–(1) A discrete representation of a number. For example, twelve, 12, XII, 1100 are four different numerals that represent the same number. (2) A numeric word that represents a number.

NUMERIC WORD–A word consisting of digits and possibly space characters and special characters.

OBJECT CODE–Output from a compiler or assembler which is itself executable machine code or is suitable for processing to produce executable machine code.

OBJECT MODULE–A module that is the output of an assembler or compiler and is input to a linkage editor.

OBJECT PROGRAM–A fully compiled or assembled program that is ready to be loaded into the computer. Synonymous with target program.

OCR–Optical Character Recognition.

OCTAL–(1) Pertaining to a characteristic or property involving a selection, choice or condition in which there are eight possibilities. (2) Pertaining to the number representation system with a radix of eight.

OCTET–A byte composed of eight bits.

OFFLINE–Pertaining to equipment or devices not under control of the central processing unit.

OFFLINE STORAGE–Storage not under control of the central processing unit.

ONES COMPLEMENT–The radix-minus-one complement in binary notation.

ONLINE–(1) Pertaining to equipment or devices under control of the central processing unit. (2) Pertaining to a user's ability to interact with a computer.

ONLINE STORAGE–Storage under control of the central processing unit.

OPENENDED–Pertaining to a process or system that can be augmented.

OPEN SUBROUTINE–A subroutine that is inserted into a routine at each place it is used.

OPERAND–That which is operated upon. An operand is usually identified by an address part of an instruction.

OPERATING SYSTEM–Software which controls the execution of computer programs and which may provide scheduling, debugging, input/output control, accounting, compilation, storage assignment, data management, and related services.

OPERATING TIME–That part of available time during which the hardware is operating and assumed to be yielding correct results. It includes development time, production time, and makeup time.

OPERATION–A program step undertaken or executed by a computer, e.g., addition, multiplication, extraction, comparison, shift, transfer. The operation is usually specified by the operator part of an instruction.

OPERATION CODE–A code that represents specific operations. Synonymous with instruction code.

OPERATION DECODER–A device that selects one or more control channels according to the operator part of a machine instruction.

OPERATOR–(1) In the description of a process, that which indicates the action to be performed on operands.

OPTICAL CHARACTER RECOGNITION–The machine identification of printed characters through use of light-sensitive devices. Abbreviated OCR.

OPTICAL SCANNER–(1) A device that scans optically and usually generates an analog or digital signal. (2) A device that optically scans printed or written data and generates their digital representations.

OR–A logic operator having the property that if P is a statement, Q is a statement, R is a statement..., then the OR of P, Q, R..., is true if at least one statement is true, false if all statements are false. P OR Q is often represented by P + Q, P V Q. Synonymous with inclusive OR, boolean add, logical add. Contrast with exclusive OR.

OR GATE–A gate that implements the logic "OR" operator.

OUTCONNECTOR–In flowcharting, a connector that indicates a point at which a flowline is broken for continuation at another point.

OUTPUT–Pertaining to a device, process, or channel involved in an output process, or to the data or states involved.

OUTPUT AREA–An area of storage reserved for output.

OUTPUT CHANNEL–A channel for conveying data from a device or logic element.

OUTPUT DATA–Data to be delivered from a device or program, usually after some processing.

OUTPUT DEVICE–The device or collective set of devices used for conveying data out of another device.

OUTPUT PROCESS–The process of delivering data by a system, subsystem, or device.

OUTPUT STATE–The state occurring on a specified output channel.

OVERFLOW–That portion of the result of an operation that exceeds the capacity of the intended unit of storage.

OVERLAY–The technique of repeatedly using the same blocks of internal storage during different stages of a program. When one routine is no longer needed in storage, another routine can replace all or part of it.

PACK–To compress data in a storage medium

by taking advantage of known characteristics of the data, in such a way that the original data can be recovered, e.g., to compress data in a storage medium by making use of bit or byte locations that would otherwise go unused.

PACKING DENSITY—The number of useful storage cells per unit of dimension, e.g., the number of bits per inch stored on a magnetic tape or drum track.

PARALLEL—Pertaining to the concurrent or simultaneous occurrence of two or more related activities in multiple devices or channels.

PARAMETER—A variable that is given a constant value for a specific purpose or process.

PARITY BIT—A check bit appended to an array of binary digits to make the sum of all the binary digits, including the check bit, always odd or always even.

PARITY CHECK—A check that tests whether the number of ones (or zeros) in an array of binary digits is odd or even.

PARTIAL CARRY—In parallel addition, a technique in which some or all of the carries are stored temporarily instead of being allowed to propagate immediately.

PASS—One cycle of processing a body of data.

PATCH—To modify a routine in a rough or expedient way.

PATTERN RECOGNITION—The identification of shapes, forms, or configurations by automatic means.

PATTERN SENSITIVE FAULT—A fault that appears in response to some particular pattern of data.

PERIPHERAL EQUIPMENT—In a data processing system, any unit of equipment, distinct from the central processing unit, which may provide the system with outside communication.

PINBOARD—A perforated board into which

pins are manually inserted to control the operation of equipment.

PLUGBOARD—A perforated board into which plugs are manually inserted to control the operation of equipment.

POSITION—In a string each location that may be occupied by a character or binary digit and may be identified by a serial number.

POSITIONAL NOTATION—A numeration system in which a number is represented by means of an ordered set of digits, such that the value contributed by each digit depends upon its position as well as upon its value.

POSTMORTEM—Pertaining to the analysis of an operation after its completion.

POSTMORTEM DUMP—A static dump, used for debugging purposes, performed at the end of a machine run.

PRECISION—The degree of discrimination with which a quantity is stated.

PREDEFINED PROCESS—A process that is identified only by name and that is defined elsewhere.

PRESET—To establish an initial condition, such as the control values of a loop.

PRESTORE—Same as initialize.

PREVENTIVE MAINTENANCE—Maintenance specifically intended to prevent faults from occurring during subsequent operation. Contrast with corrective maintenance. Corrective maintenance and preventive maintenance are both performed during maintenance time.

PREVENTIVE MAINTENANCE TIME—Time, usually scheduled, used to perform preventive maintenance.

PROBLEM DESCRIPTION—(1) In information processing, a statement of a problem. The statement may also include a description of the method of solution, the procedures and algorithms, etc. (2) A statement of a problem. The statement may also include a description of the method of solution, the solution itself, the transformations of data and the relationship of procedures, data, constraints, and environment.

PROBLEM ORIENTED LANGUAGE—A programming language designed for the convenient expression of a given class of problems.

PROCESS—A systematic sequence of operations to produce a specified result.

PROCESSOR—(1) In hardware, a data processor. (2) In software, a computer program that includes the compiling, assembling, translating, and related functions for a specific programming language.

PROGRAM—(1) A series of actions proposed in order to achieve a certain result. (2) Loosely, a routine. (3) To design, write, and test a program as in (1). (4) Loosely, to write a routine.

PROGRAM LIBRARY—A collection of available computer programs and routines.

PROGRAM SENSITIVE FAULT—A fault that appears in response to some particular sequence of program steps.

PROGRAMMER—A person mainly involved in designing, writing and testing computer programs.

PROGRAMMING—The design, the writing, and testing of a program.

PROGRAMMING FLOWCHART—A flowchart representing the sequence of operations in a program.

PROGRAMMING LANGUAGE—A language used to prepare computer programs.

PROGRAMMING MODULE—A discrete identifiable set of instructions, usually handled as a unit, by an assembler, a compiler, a linkage editor, a loading routine, or other type of routine or subroutine.

PULSE REPETITION RATE—The number of pulses per unit time.

PUNCH—A perforation, as in a punched card or paper tape.

PUNCHED CARD—A card punched with a pattern of holes to represent data.

PUNCHED TAPE—A tape on which a pattern of holes or cuts is used to represent data.

PUNCH POSITION—A defined location on a card or tape where a hole may be punched.

QUANTIZE—To subdivide the range of values of a variable into a finite number of nonoverlapping, but not necessarily equal, subranges or intervals, each of which is represented by an assigned value within the subrange.

RADIAL TRANSFER—An input process, or an output process.

RADIX—In positional representation, that integer, if it exists, by which the significance of the digit place must be multiplied to give the significance of the next higher digit place.

RADIX COMPLEMENT—A complement obtained by subtracting each digit from one less than its radix, then adding one to the least significant digit, executing all carries required.

RADIX-MINUS-ONE COMPLEMENT—A complement obtained by subtracting each digit from one less than the radix.

RADIX NOTATION—A positional representation in which the significance of any two adjacent digit positions has an integral ratio called the radix of the less significant of the two positions; permissible values of the digit in any position range from zero to one less than the radix of that position.

RADIX POINT—In radix notation, the real or implied character that separates the digits associated with the integral part of a numeral from those associated with the fractional part.

RANDOM ACCESS—An access mode in which specific logical records are obtained from or placed into a mass storage file in a nonsequential manner.

RANDOM NUMBERS—A series of numbers obtained by chance.

READ—To acquire or interpret data from a storage device, a data medium, or any other source.

REAL TIME—Pertaining to the actual time during which a physical process transpires.

REAL TIME INPUT—Input data inserted into a system at the time of generation by another system.

REAL TIME OUTPUT—Output data removed from a system at time of need by another system.

RECORD—A collection of related items of data, treated as a unit, for example, one line of an invoice may form a record; a complete set of such records may form a file.

RECORD GAP—An area on a data medium used to indicate the end of a block or record.

RECORDING DENSITY—The number of bits in single linear track measured per unit of length of the recording medium.

RECORD LAYOUT—The arrangement and structure of data in a record, including the sequence and size of its components. By extension, a record layout might be the description thereof.

RECORD LENGTH—A measure of the size of a record, usually specified in units such as words or characters.

REGISTER—A device capable of storing a specified amount of data such as one word.

REGISTRATION—The accurate positioning relative to a reference.

RELATIVE ADDRESS—The number that specifies the difference between the absolute address and the base address.

RELATIVE CODING—Coding that uses machine instructions with relative addresses.

RELIABILITY—The probability that a device will perform without failure for a specified time period or amount of usage.

RELOCATE—In computer programming, to move a routine from one portion of storage to another and to adjust the necessary address references so that the routine, in its new location, can be executed.

REMOTE ACCESS—Pertaining to communication with a data processing facility by one or more stations that are distant from that facility.

REMOTE STATION—Data terminal equipment for communicating with a data processing system from a location that is time, space, or electrically distant.

REPERFORATOR—REceiving PERFORATOR.

REPETITION INSTRUCTION—An instruction that causes one or more instructions to be executed an indicated number of times.

RESET—(1) To restore a storage device to a prescribed initial state, not necessarily that denoting zero. (2) To place a binary cell into the state denoting zero.

RESTART—To reestablish the execution of a routine, using the data recorded at a checkpoint.

RIGHT-JUSTIFY—(1) To adjust the printing positions of characters on a page so that the right margin of the page is regular. (2) To shift the contents of a register so that the least significant digit is at some specified position of the register.

ROUNDING ERROR—An error due to roundoff.

ROUNDOFF—To delete the least significant digit or digits of a numeral, and to adjust the part retained in accordance with some rule.

ROUTINE—An ordered set of instructions that may have some general or frequent use.

ROW—A horizontal arrangement of characters or other expressions.

ROW BINARY—Pertaining to the binary representation of data on cards in which the significances of punch positions are assigned along the card rows. For example, each row in an 80-column card may be used to represent 80 consecutive binary digits.

RUN—A single, continuous performance of a computer program or routine.

SCALE—To adjust the representation of a quantity by a factor in order to bring its range within prescribed limits.

SCALE FACTOR—A number used as a multiplier, so chosen that it will cause a set of quantities to fall within a given range of values.

SCAN—To examine sequentially, part by part.

SCHEDULED MAINTENANCE—Maintenance carried out in accordance with an established plan.

SEARCH—To examine a set of items for one or more having a desired property.

SEGMENT—(1) To divide a computer program into parts such that the program can be executed without the entire program being in internal storage at any one time. (2) A part of a computer program as in (1).

SELECTION CHECK—A check that verifies the choice of devices, such as registers, in the execution of an instruction.

SELECTIVE DUMP—A dump of one or more specified storage locations.

SEQUENCE—An arrangement of items according to a specified set of rules.

SEQUENTIAL—Pertaining to the occurrence of events in time sequence, with little or no simultaneity or overlap of events.

SEQUENTIAL CONTROL—Defined sequence until a different sequence is explicitly initiated by a jump instruction.

SEQUENTIAL LOGIC ELEMENT—A device having at least one output channel and one or more input channels, all characterized by discrete states, such that the state of each output channel is determined by the previous states

of the input channels.

SEQUENTIAL OPERATION—Pertaining to the performance of operations one after the other.

SERIAL—(1) Pertaining to the sequential or consecutive occurrence of two or more related activities in a single device or channel.

SET—(1) A collection. (2) To place a storage device into a specified state, usually other than that denoting zero or space character. (3) To place a binary cell into the state denoting one.

SETUP—(1) In a computer which consists of an assembly of individual computing units, the arrangement of interconnections between the units, and the adjustments needed for the computer to solve a particular problem. (2) An arrangement of data or devices to solve a particular problem.

SETUP DIAGRAM—A diagram specifying a given computer setup.

SEXADECIMAL—(1) Pertaining to a characteristic or property involving a selection, choice, or condition in which there are sixteen possibilities. (2) Pertaining to the numeration system with a radix of sixteen. Synonymous with hexadecimal.

SHIFT—A movement of data to the right or left.

SHIFT REGISTER—A register in which the stored data can be moved to the right or left.

SIGN BIT—A binary digit occupying the sign position.

SIGN DIGIT—A digit occupying the sign position.

SIGNIFICANCE—In positional representation, the factor, dependent on the digit place, by which a digit is multiplied to obtain its additive contribution in the representation of a number.

SIGNIFICANT DIGIT—A digit that is needed for a certain purpose, particularly one that must be kept to preserve a specific accuracy or precision.

SIGN POSITION—A position, normally located at one end of a numeral, that contains an indication of the algebraic sign of the number.

SKEW—The angular displacement of a symbol or data medium from the intended or ideal placement.

SKIP—To ignore one or more instructions in a sequence of instructions.

SMOOTH—To apply procedures that decrease or eliminate rapid fluctuations in data.

SNAPSHOT DUMP—A selective dynamic dump performed at various points in a machine run.

SOFTWARE—A set of computer programs, procedures, and possibly associated documentation concerned with the operation of a data processing system, e.g., compilers, library routines, manuals, circuit diagrams.

SOLID STATE COMPONENT—A component whose operation depends on the control of electric or magnetic phenomena in solids, e.g., a transistor, crystal diode, ferrite core.

SORT—(1) To segregate items into groups according to some definite rules. (2) Same as order.

SORTER—A person, device, or computer routine that sorts.

SOURCE LANGUAGE—The language from which a statement is translated.

SOURCE PROGRAM—A computer program written in a source language.

SPECIAL CHARACTER—A graphic character that is neither a letter, nor a digit, nor a space character.

SPECIAL PURPOSE COMPUTER—A computer that is designed to handle a restricted class of problems.

SPOT PUNCH—A device for punching one hole at a time.

STATIC DUMP—A dump that is performed at a particular point in time with respect to a machine at the end of a run.

STORAGE—(1) Pertaining to a device into which data can be entered, in which they can be held, and from which they can be retrieved at a later time. (2) Loosely, any device that can store data. (3) Synonymous with memory.

STORAGE ALLOCATION—The assignment of blocks of data to specified blocks of storage.

STORAGE CAPACITY—The amount of data that can be continued in a storage device.

STORAGE CELL—An elementary unit of storage.

STORAGE DEVICE—A device into which data can be inserted, in which they can be retained, and from which they can be retrieved.

STORAGE PROTECTION—An arrangement for preventing access to storage for either reading, or writing, or both.

STORE—(1) To enter data into a storage device. (2) To retain data in a storage device.

STORED PROGRAM COMPUTER—A computer controlled by internally stored instructions that can synthesize, store, and in some cases alter instructions as though they were data and that can subsequently execute these instructions.

SUBROUTINE—A routine that can be part of another routine.

SUBROUTINE CALL—The subroutine, in object coding, that performs the call function.

SWITCH—A device or programming technique for making a selection, e.g., a toggle, a conditional jump.

SYMBOL—A representation of something by reason of relationship, association, or convention.

SYMBOLIC ADDRESS—An address expressed in symbols convenient to the computer programmer.

SYMBOLIC CODING—Coding that uses machine instructions with symbolic addresses.

SYMBOLIC LOGIC—The discipline that treats formal logic by means of a formalized artificial language or symbolic calculus, whose purpose is to avoid the ambiguities and logical inadequacies of natural languages.

SYMBOL STRING—A string consisting solely of symbols.

SYNCHRONIZATION PULSES—Pulses introduced by transmitting equipment into the receiving equipment to keep the two equipments operating in step.

SYNTAX—(1) The structure of expressions in a language. (2) The rules governing the structure of a language.

SYSTEM—An organized collection of men, machines, and methods required to accomplish a set of specific functions.

TABLE—A collection of data in which each item is uniquely identified by a label, by its position relative to the other items, or by some other means.

TAPE DRIVE—A device that moves tape past a head.

TAPE TO CARD—Pertaining to equipment or methods that transmit data from either magnetic tape or punched tape to punched cards.

TAPE TRANSPORT—Same as tape drive.

TAPE UNIT—A device containing a tape drive, together with reading, and writing heads and associated controls.

TEMPORARY STORAGE—In programming, storage locations reserved for intermediate results. Synonymous with working storage.

TERMINAL—A point in a system or communication network at which data can either enter or leave.

THIN FILM—Loosely, magnetic thin film.

TIME SHARE—To use a device for two or more interleaved purposes.

TIME SHARING—Pertaining to the interleaved use of the time of a device.

TOGGLE—(1) Same as flip-flop. (2) Pertaining to any device having two stable states.

TRACING ROUTINE—A routine that provides a historical record of specified events in the execution of a program.

TRACK—The portion of a moving storage medium, such as a drum, tape, or disc, that is accessible to a given reading head position.

TRANSFORM—To change the form of data according to specific rules.

TRANSLATE—To transform statements from one language to another without significantly changing the meaning.

TRANSMISSION—(1) The sending of data from one location and the receiving of data in another location, usually leaving the source data unchanged. (2) The sending of data.

TRANSMIT—To send data from one location and to receive the data at another location.

TROUBLESHOOT—Same as debug.

TRUNCATE—To terminate a computational process in accordance with some rule, e.g., to end the evaluation of a power series at a specified term.

TRUNCATION ERROR—An error due to truncation.

TRUTH TABLE—A table that describes a logic function by listing all possible combinations of input values and indicating, for each combination, the true output values.

TWELVE PUNCH—A punch in the top row of a Hollerith punch card. Synonymous with y-punch.

TWO-OUT-OF-FIVE CODE—A positional notation in which each decimal digit is represented by five binary digits of which two are one kind (e.g., ones) and three are the other kind (e.g., zeros).

TWOS COMPLEMENT—The radix complement in binary notation.

TYPE FONT—Type of a given size and style, e.g., 10-point Bodoni Modern.

UNIT—(1) A device having a special function. (2) A basic element.

UNPACK—To recover the original data from packed data.

UTILITY ROUTINE—Same as service routine.

VARIABLE—A quantity that can assume any of a given set of values.

VARIABLE-LENGTH RECORD—Pertaining to a file in which the records are not uniform in length.

VARIABLE-POINT REPRESENTATION—A positional representation in which the position of the radix point is explicitly indicated by a special character at that position.

VENN DIAGRAM—A diagram in which sets are represented by closed regions.

VERIFY—(1) To determine whether a transcription of data or other operation has been accomplished accurately. (2) To check the results of keypunching.

VOLATILE STORAGE—A storage device in which stored data are lost when the applied power is removed, e.g., an acoustic delay line.

WEIGHT—Same as significance.

WORD—(1) A character string or a bit string considered as an entity. (2) See alphabetic word, computer word, half-word, machine word, numeric word.

WORD LENGTH—A measure of the size of a word, usually specified in units such as characters or binary digits.

WRITE—To record data in a storage device or a data medium. The recording need not be permanent, such as the writing on a cathode ray tube display device.

X-PUNCH—Same as eleven-punch.

Y-PUNCH—Same as twelve-punch.

ZEROFILL—To character fill with the representation of zero.

ZERO SUPPRESSION—The elimination of non-significant zeros in a numeral.

ZONE PUNCH—A punch in the eleven, twelve, or zero row of a punched card.